LEONARDO DA VINCI
THE DIVINE AND THE GROTESQUE

MARTIN CLAYTON

THE ROYAL COLLECTION

This publication has been generously supported by

This book accompanies the Royal Collection exhibition
which will be shown at The Queen's Gallery, Holyroodhouse,
Edinburgh, 30 November 2002–30 March 2003, and at
The Queen's Gallery, Buckingham Palace, London,
9 May–9 November 2003.

Published by
Royal Collection Enterprises Ltd
St James's Palace, London SW1A 1JR

For a complete catalogue of current publications, please write
to the address above, or visit our website on www.royal.gov.uk

118208 (hardback)
118190 (paperback)

ISBN (hardback) 1 902163 97 4
ISBN (paperback) 1 902163 09 5

British Library Cataloguing in Publication Data
A catalogue record for this book is available from the
British Library.

Designed by Sally McIntosh
Produced by Book Production Consultants plc, Cambridge
Printed and bound by Conti Tipocolor

Front cover: LEONARDO DA VINCI, *The bust of a man, full face,
and the head of a lion, c.*1505–10 (CAT. 22, detail)
Back cover: LEONARDO DA VINCI, *A man tricked by Gypsies, c.*1493
(CAT. 41, detail)
Frontispiece: LEONARDO DA VINCI, *The head of St Anne, c.*1510–15
(CAT. 56, detail)

CONTENTS

An Outline of Leonardo's Life

AND THE PROVENANCE OF THE WINDSOR DRAWINGS

1452	15 APRIL: Born at Anchiano, near Vinci, Tuscany
1469	Probably moves to Florence and enters the studio of Andrea del Verrocchio
1472	Member of the Company of St Luke (painters' guild)
c.1473–6	Paints the *Annunciation* (Florence, Uffizi) and *Ginevra de' Benci* (Washington, National Gallery of Art)
1476	Still in Verrocchio's studio
1478	JANUARY: Commission for an altarpiece for the Palazzo della Signoria, Florence (not executed)
1481	MARCH: Commission for the *Adoration of the Magi* (Uffizi)
	SEPTEMBER: Last payment for the *Adoration of the Magi*
c.1482	Moves to Milan. Paints *St Jerome* (Vatican, Pinacoteca)
1483	APRIL: Commission for the *Virgin of the Rocks* (Paris, Louvre)
c.1483–90	Enters service of Ludovico Sforza. Paints portraits of a *Musician* (Milan, Ambrosiana) and *Cecilia Gallerani* (Krakow, Museo Czartoryski)
1487–90	Engaged in architectural work in Milan and Pavia. First anatomical studies
c.1489–93	At work on Sforza monument. Intense work on proportion and the grotesque
c.1494–7	Paints the *Last Supper* (Milan, Santa Maria delle Grazie); probably begins second version of the *Virgin of the Rocks* (London, National Gallery)
1499	DECEMBER: Leaves Milan
1500	FEBRUARY: In Mantua. Draws portrait of *Isabella d'Este* (Louvre)
	MARCH: In Venice, then to Florence
1501	In Florence. At work on the *Madonna of the Yarnwinder* (priv. coll.) and a cartoon of the *Madonna and Child with St Anne*
1502–3	Architect, engineer and mapmaker to Cesare Borgia
1503	Back in Florence
	OCTOBER: Begins cartoon of the *Battle of Anghiari* (destroyed)
1504–6	At work on the *Battle of Anghiari*; designs *Leda and the swan* (destroyed) and begins work on *Mona Lisa* (Louvre). Studies of bird-flight and geometry
1506–7	Travels repeatedly between Florence and Milan
1507–8	WINTER: Dissects centenarian in hospital of Santa Maria Nuova, Florence
1508–13	Studies of anatomy and water. Produces designs for Trivulzio monument. Probably begins panel of the *Madonna and Child with St Anne* (Louvre)

1513	SEPTEMBER: Leaves Milan
	DECEMBER: In Rome, in service of Giuliano de' Medici
1516	AUGUST: Last record of presence in Rome
1517–19	In service of Francis I in France. Right hand paralysed. Produces architectural and geometrical studies, designs for masquerades and an equestrian monument. Assistants working on the *Madonna and Child with St Anne*
1519	2 MAY: Dies at Amboise. Leonardo's drawings bequeathed to Francesco Melzi, paintings to Salaì, both of whom return to Milan
1524	Death of Salaì
*c.*1570	Death of Melzi
1580s	Acquisition of Leonardo's papers from Melzi's heirs by Pompeo Leoni
1608	Death of Pompeo Leoni in Madrid; his collection dispersed
by 1630	Leoni album in England, in collection of Earl of Arundel
1646	Death of Arundel in Padua. Whereabouts of Leoni album unknown
1690	Leoni album in Royal Collection at Kensington Palace

A Note on Leonardo's Drawings and Manuscripts

The Royal Library at Windsor Castle holds by far the largest surviving group of Leonardo's 'artistic' and anatomical drawings, some 600 sheets in all. These were all catalogued in Clark and Pedretti 1968–9, and are here referred to by their Royal Library inventory numbers ('RL'). The first three volumes of a projected series of facsimile catalogues of the Windsor drawings have also been published; drawings in the present volume can be found in Keele and Pedretti 1979 and in Pedretti 1987. Two other compendia of Leonardo's papers survive: the Codex Atlanticus in the Biblioteca Ambrosiana, Milan (this volume was refoliated in the late twentieth century, but the sheets are here referred to following their old foliation); and the Codex Arundel in the British Library, London.

Leonardo's individual notebooks are held in the Bibliothèque de l'Institut de France, Paris (twelve lettered as Paris MSS A-M and two known from a former owner as Codex Ashburnham I and II); the Biblioteca Nacional, Madrid (Madrid MSS I and II); the Victoria and Albert Museum, London (Codex Forster I-III); and in the Biblioteca Trivulziana in Milan, the Biblioteca Reale in Turin, and the Bill Gates collection, Seattle (not referred to in this book).

Three volumes containing copies of Leonardo's notes and drawings are of particular importance to this book. These are the Codex Urbinas in the Biblioteca Apostolica, Vatican City, an attempt by Francesco Melzi to construct Leonardo's *Treatise on Painting*; the Codex Huygens in the Pierpont Morgan Library, New York, a volume on proportion and perspective assembled by Carlo Urbino in 1569; and an edition of Rabelais, in the New York Public Library, into which is inserted a sequence of mid-sixteenth-century copies of Leonardo's grotesques, known as the Spencer Album.

The loose drawings in other collections are referred to by the inventory numbers of their respective museums. All works are on white paper unless otherwise stated. Height precedes width in measurements. Comparative figures are of works in the Royal Library unless otherwise stated.

INTRODUCTION

If the painter wishes to see beauties that charm him, it lies in his power to create them;
and if he wishes to see monstrosities that are frightful, buffoonish or ridiculous, or pitiable,
he can be lord and god thereof.[1]

Leonardo da Vinci wrote at length about the power of the artist to create an internal fantasy in which the physical world is transformed at will. Drawing was his principal means of exploring the phenomenal world and the boundless possibilities of the imagination: 'simple natural forms are finite, but the works which our hands perform at the command of the eye are infinite.'[2] The counterpart of Leonardo's obsessive observation of reality was a desire to transform that reality.

Leonardo's studies of heads, in their many forms, are among the most striking works in this oeuvre of unequalled variety. Some were preparatory studies for his paintings; many more were independent investigations of the human face, a motif that carries more meaning for us, at a more fundamental level, than any other subject available to the artist. A likeness can be adequately captured by a single profile line, and though so simple in essence, the form of the face is central to our interaction with the world – our perception of the emotions of others, our friendships and loves, and the reciprocal responses that others have to us. Leonardo's inexhaustible fascination with the face, with our reactions to its beauty or ugliness, and with the wider issues of the body as a whole and its adornments, is central to an understanding of his art.

The idea that physical appearance is somehow indicative of intelligence or moral worth is ingrained in our modes of thought. From ancient times (and most influentially in the writings of Plato), the soul was held to determine all aspects of the individual, and thus character and emotion were related fundamentally to the physical form of the body. Physical beauty reflected spiritual beauty, and deformity or ugliness were the signs of an unbalanced constitution and moral turpitude. To the modern mind, such a notion seems absurd; nonetheless, the consequences for the artist are obvious. A beautiful body houses a beautiful soul: the Madonna, for instance, is always depicted as beautiful, and the evil or corrupt have always been portrayed as ugly or deformed. An inconsistency arose in the representation of haggard saints and prophets, but in such cases the very absence of beauty could itself be a sign of virtue, testifying to a life spent in the rejection of vanity. This coexistence of external ugliness and internal grace was facilitated by the distinction drawn by theologians of the Middle Ages between the beauty of the world, perceived by the senses, and the beauty of God, perceived by the mind. These were barely comparable: the beauty of a natural object could lead to a meditation on the splendour of God as revealed through his creations, but the transient material world was trivial beside the eternal beauties of harmony and moral order that were the true form of the universe.[3]

Beauty was therefore universally equated with harmony – musical harmony, simple arithmetical relationships in the structure of the cosmos (the 'music of the spheres'), a harmonious arrangement of the parts of a face, a body, or a composition; conversely, ugliness was the disharmony or inappropriateness of these parts. A note by an associate of Leonardo summarised this:

> Monstrous is that which has a huge head and short legs; and monstrous is that which with rich clothes is of great poverty; and thus we say that well-proportioned is that in which the parts are in correspondence with the whole.[4]

This simple formula covers the whole range of material in this catalogue; and yet it provides little practical guidance for the artist, as it merely replaces the problem of defining 'beauty' with the problem of defining 'well-proportioned'.

The codification of perfect proportion in the human body was therefore one of the first subjects to engage Leonardo when he began to assemble material for a projected treatise on painting in the late 1480s (CATS. 2–5). At the same time Leonardo made a complementary investigation into the negation of beauty, distorting the proportions of the face to create visions of 'perfect ugliness'. These two antitheses of beauty had been latent in Leonardo's art from the outset, but once he began to study them in an explicit manner, their duality emerged as one of the central themes of his career.

Leonardo's wish to cover in his treatise everything of concern to the painter prevented him from ever completing the work. Instead, after around 1490, the theoretical issues considered in his notes developed in tandem with the themes explored in his paintings and drawings. Therefore it is sometimes difficult to distinguish between those drawings that were explorations of form for its own sake and those that were practical studies for Leonardo's artistic projects – not just his paintings (CATS. 51–61) but the whole range of activity that occupied Leonardo during his career, such as the costume designs catalogued here (CATS. 64–75).

Leonardo insisted repeatedly in his notes that the artist must strive to paint figures whose actions and expressions reveal their character and their emotions; on the verso of CAT. 26, for instance, he stated 'when you make a figure, think well about what it is and what you want it to do, and see that the work is in keeping with the figure's aim and character.' This concern with appropriateness, or 'decorum', is found throughout Renaissance theories on art (and on much else besides), having first been codified by Leon Battista Alberti in his seminal work *On Painting*,[5] written in 1435 and the principal model for Leonardo's own projected treatise. The classically educated Alberti had styled many of his theories on ancient treatises on rhetoric, especially the works of Cicero and Quintilian, which held that the aim of rhetoric (and thus, by extension, art) was to engage and thus move the listener (or viewer). This should be done by choosing a style fitting to the subject-matter, with a variety of suitable motifs, changes of tone and pace, and so on. Leonardo's studies of heads for his paintings, therefore, are attempts to arrive at appropriate physical types and expressions, and on at least one occasion – the preparatory work towards the *Last Supper* – he identified individuals who might be suitable models for the characters he had to depict (see p. 129).

Leonardo's independent head studies, however, are rarely concerned with the representation of character or emotion. He rejected the predictive basis of physiognomics, accepting only that characteristic expressions gradually imprint themselves on the features:

> The face shows some indications of the nature of men, their vices and their complexions; in the face the marks which separate the cheeks from the lips, the nostrils from the nose, and the sockets from the eyes, show clearly whether these are cheerful men, often laughing; and those who show few such indications are men who engage in thought; and those, the planes of whose features are in great reliefs and hollows are bestial and angry men, of little reason; and those who have very clearly marked lines between the eyebrows are irascible; and those who have horizontal lines marked on their foreheads are men full of concealed or public lamentations; and similar things can be said of many parts of the face.[6]

It has often been assumed that the standard forms examined in 'Ideal Types' (CATS. 15–25), and more particularly the comic-grotesques in 'The Grotesque' (CATS. 26–41), are relics of a systematic investigation into the relationship between facial type and character, or expression and emotion, and even that Leonardo had composed a treatise on the subject.[7] One drawing here (CAT. 22) does compare the heads of a man and a lion in a way that relates directly to contemporary physiognomic theory, and the opposed profiles in a few of Leonardo's drawings have been seen by some scholars as illustrations of humoral types – melancholic, choleric and so on (see CAT. 27).

But the ideal types and the non-narrative grotesques were, on the whole, studies in pure form, and the drawings are too heterogeneous for it to be contended that they are illustrations of a coherent theory or even explorations of a common theme. This must explain why not one of the many attempts to explain Leonardo's drawings of heads in terms of some overarching scheme has been at all convincing.

A distorted perception of Leonardo's interests can be traced to the mid-sixteenth century, barely a generation after his death. Surrounded by countless copies, prints and pastiches of Leonardo's drawings of heads and monstrosities, Giorgio Vasari (in his biography of 1550, expanded in 1568) and Gian Paolo Lomazzo (in his treatises of 1584 and 1590) were primarily responsible for the later vision of Leonardo as a bizarre genius. Their tales of his practical jokes, of following odd-looking people in the streets to commit their likenesses to memory and of organising picnics for peasants or visiting condemned prisoners to observe their facial expressions, all fed a later sixteenth-century taste (especially strong in Milan, where Leonardo had produced many of his grotesque inventions) for a genre of robust comic art that seemed to have Leonardo's imprimatur. The abundance of his inventions in this vein and the greatness of his reputation gave his followers scope to expand upon this variety, and much of the discussion ostensibly on Leonardo and comic art has focused instead on his followers.[8]

By the start of the following century, the great majority of Leonardo's original drawings of heads had left Italy for Spain with the sculptor Pompeo Leoni, who had bought the bulk of Leonardo's surviving papers from the heirs of Leonardo's pupil Francesco Melzi. After Leoni's death in 1608 his albums of Leonardo drawings were auctioned, and one, containing the drawings now at Windsor, found its way to England, where it entered the collection of Thomas Howard, 2nd Earl of Arundel. While in Arundel's collection, Leonardo's drawings were eagerly copied by contemporary artists and many were etched by Wenceslaus Hollar (FIG. 1), and it is revealing that a far higher proportion of the head studies were reproduced than any other category of drawing.[9] A century later, sixty small copies in an album owned by Pierre-Jean Mariette (now in the Louvre) were reproduced in etchings by the Comte de Caylus, in the *Recueil de Testes de caractere & de Charges* of 1730 (FIG. 2).[10] Leonardo's reputation and the popularity of these prints of the head studies were mutually reinforcing.

Before Jean Paul Richter's groundbreaking study of Leonardo's notebooks,[11] first published in 1883, the head studies were thus a more significant component of Leonardo's reputation than the totality of his scientific studies. Only from the late nineteenth century did our comprehension of Leonardo's achievements move substantially beyond editions of the unfinished *Treatise*, the heads, and a handful of his paintings (with many more woeful misattributions) to give us the fully rounded picture of 'Leonardo the Renaissance man' that we enjoy today.[12] We can now see the head studies in the context of Leonardo's vision of the world and his aims as an artist; but for almost four centuries after his death, the universal perception of Leonardo's art could in large part have been summed up by the title of this book, the Divine and the Grotesque.

1. Codex Urbinas, f. 5r; Richter 1939, no. 19.

2. Codex Urbinas f. 16r; Richter 1939, p. 68, no. 31.

3. For a good introduction to medieval aesthetics see Eco 1986; the situation in Leonardo's day is summarised in Hemsoll 1998.

4. Codex Atlanticus, f. 375r-b, c. This note is not in Leonardo's hand but is on a page used by him for other studies, and must have been jotted down by a workshop colleague.

5. Alberti 1972. On Leonardo and Alberti see Zoubov 1960, and Mantua 1994 *passim*.

6. Codex Urbinas, f. 109v; McMahon 1956, no. 425.

7. See Kwakkelstein 1993b and 1994.

8. See Meijer 1971; Miedema 1977; Bora 1989; Migliaccio 1995; Paliaga 1995b.

9. See Roberts (forthcoming) for an account of the arrival and reception of the Leonardo volume in England.

10. See Steinitz 1974.

11. Richter 1939.

12. See especially Turner 1993.

FIG. 1 *(above)*
WENCESLAUS HOLLAR (1607–77), after Leonardo
*A grotesque couple, c.*1645
Etching, plate 7.7 × 11.9 cm (3¹⁄₁₆ × 4¹¹⁄₁₆″)

FIG. 2
ANNE-CLAUDE-PHILIPPE DE TUBIÈRES,
LE COMTE DE CAYLUS (1692–1765), after Leonardo
A caricature of Dante, from *Recueil de Testes de caractere
& de Charges,* Paris 1730
Etching, plate 9.9 × 10.1 cm (3⁷⁄₈ × 4″)

THE PROFILE SHEET

1

LEONARDO DA VINCI
Recto: *The Madonna and Child with the
infant Baptist, and heads in profile, c.*1478
Verso: *Heads in profile*

Pen and ink, 40.2 × 29.0 cm (15¹³⁄₁₆ × 11⁷⁄₁₆″)
RL 12276

The two sides of this sheet present a conspectus of many of the themes treated in this book. The large compositional sketch of the Madonna and Child with the infant Baptist was the first drawing to be made on the recto, filling almost the whole sheet. Leonardo drew the head of the Madonna in two positions, first looking down at the suckling Child and then, more heavily hatched, gazing sombrely at an indeterminate point between the viewer and the holy group. Leonardo added another smaller study of the Baptist at upper right, and two sketches of figures in a pose familiar from Roman sarcophagi, with front leg bent and rear leg outstretched. He then covered the two sides of the sheet with twenty-four human heads and three heads of animals.

The roaring of the lion and dragon at the bottom of the recto have their human counterpart in a sketch towards the upper left of the verso. The lion is little different, except in drawing style, from that on a sheet of twenty-five years later (CAT. 47) – Leonardo's subjects rarely show emotion, and when they do it is usually this open-mouthed anger. His main interest was in the permanent rather than the fleeting, and all but one of the other studies on this sheet show the face in impassive right profile. Being left-handed, most of Leonardo's profiles face to the right – it is natural for a draughtsman to construct a profile with his hand 'inside' the face.

Leonardo maintained a marked preference for the profile in his drawings throughout his career. The profile reduces the face to elements that can be manipulated at will, and while it might appear that Leonardo was working here on three facial types – young man, young woman, old man – all the profiles are in fact variants of a form that was standard in his art. At the lower centre of the recto, just above the dragon's head, is a pure profile drawn with a mouth but no eye. This is Leonardo's 'neutral' profile, with no distortions or exaggerations – the archetype of beauty. A couple of the other studies come close to it, such as the carefully finished head of the youth below the Child at centre left, the woman at top left, or the youth at upper centre of the verso. All the other heads are essentially variations on that profile, in which the artist changed the shape of one or other of the components to observe the effects. Leonardo was investigating, unsystematically, how subtle variations in the shapes of forehead, nose, mouth and chin affect our perception of the face's age, gender, and beauty. At lower right, for example, the profile progresses through three stages of transformation as the line of the nose becomes more undulating and the lips more puckered. Just below the centre, an old man with drooping nose and jutting lower lip is contrasted with an infant with turned-up nose and receding lip. The woman at top left is caricatured (see p. 74 for a discussion of this term) in another profile, immediately adjacent, in which all her features are swollen somewhat, though she may have changed gender in the process.

CAT. I (verso)

On the verso at centre left is the warrior type who was to be a constantly recurring motif in Leonardo's art. A very similarly drawn profile appears on a sheet in the Uffizi in Florence, inscribed by Leonardo with the date 1478, and the present sheet must have been executed at around the same time. This face is distorted one stage further in the profile to the right of top left, as the nose descends and the lower lip rises almost to meet it.

Most of these profiles must have been drawn from Leonardo's imagination, though several of the sketches of the young woman show her in contemporary dress and may have been drawn from the life. Like all artists of his day, Leonardo doubtless used friends, assistants and servants as impromptu models, but here the young woman was no more than raw material for Leonardo's game of profiles, losing any sense of individuality and becoming just a type. When Leonardo looked hard at a model he was capable of great objectivity (CAT. 43), but here we see how early in his career this one basic profile with its range of variations had become habitual. It would be possible to rearrange the profiles on this sheet into a gradually evolving sequence, from the ideally beautiful to the ideally ugly – from the divine to the grotesque – and this locus was to be the basis of all of Leonardo's investigations into the form of the face.

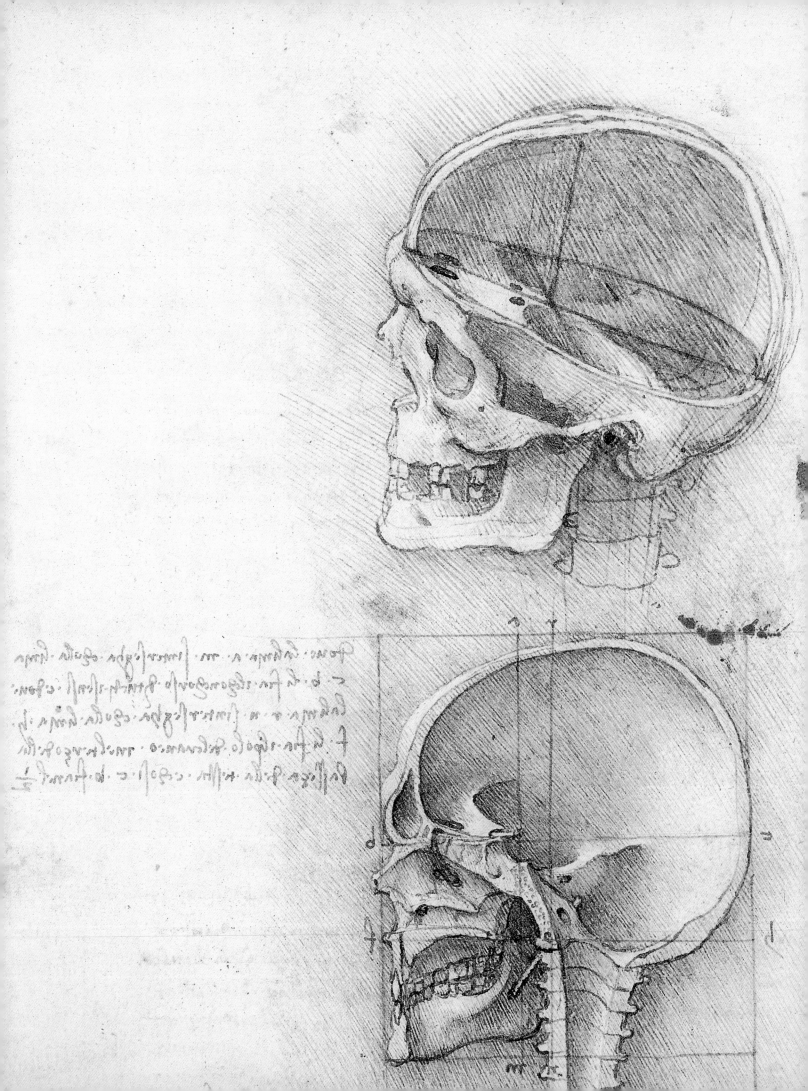

THE DIVINE BODY

It was realised at an early date in human history – at least by the time of Pythagoras in the sixth century BC – that the musical notes made by strings whose lengths were in simple numeric ratios sounded pleasing together. This concept was easily extended to spatial intervals, and established the principle that harmonic ratios were intrinsically 'right' and thus fundamental to the structure of the universe. Leonardo understood this analogy:

> From painting which serves the eye, the noblest sense, arises harmony of proportions, just as many different voices joined together and singing simultaneously produces a harmonic proportion.[1]

Such proportions were held to be beautiful in themselves, independent of any observer, and were instinctively recognised as beautiful because man was seen as a microcosm, reflecting the structure of the cosmos in his own body. An aesthetic expression of this idea was apparently formulated in the fifth century BC by the Greek sculptor Polykleitos, who defined perfect beauty as the mutual harmony of all the parts, such that nothing can be added, subtracted or altered but for the worse. This became a commonplace of artistic theory in the Classical period, but it did not address the definition of this harmony. A formulation of the numerical ratios between the dimensions of the ideal human body was needed.

We do not know how many alternative proportional systems were developed in Classical times, as only one extensive treatise on the arts survived the Dark Ages, Vitruvius' *De architectura*, written in the first century BC. The pre-eminence of Vitruvius' proportional system during the Renaissance was due entirely to this accident of survival.

Vitruvius discussed human proportion in the context of architectural proportion: just like a well-designed and harmonious building, the body should be divisible into equal units, and all its measurements should be expressible either in terms of that unit or as simple fractions of the whole. Vitruvius also stated that the body when standing with arms outstretched fits into a square and, with all limbs splayed, into a circle centred on the navel. This fit of the human body with the perfect forms of the circle and the square was an inevitable consequence of the perfection and harmony of the universe.

During the Middle Ages there appears to have been more knowledge of Vitruvius in northern Europe than in Italy, which was almost oblivious to *De architectura* until the poet and scholar Petrarch brought a manuscript from France around 1350. The circulation of copies of the treatise grew dramatically during the fifteenth century, due in part to Leon Battista Alberti's sustained interest in the text and his emulation of it in his own *De re aedificatoria* (finished in 1452 and published in 1485). The first printed edition of Vitruvius was published in Rome between 1486 and 1492, and the first fully illustrated edition by Fra Giocondo in Venice in 1511.

Vitruvius' harmonic system did not go unchallenged in the Renaissance, for an alternative evolved in the High Middle Ages from a separate Hellenistic tradition, known as the pseudo-Varronian system. In some ways this was a more sophisticated system than Vitruvius', as it divided the body in a non-regular manner derived from measurement, but this very lack of regularity must have detracted from its appeal. In his treatise *De statua* (c.1443–52) Alberti himself also attempted to move away from the harmonic system, instead dividing each foot into 10 *unceolae* and 100 *minutae* – a decimal system that reached its final expression in the metre of the Enlightenment. Vitruvius nonetheless remained the authority for all Early Renaissance considerations of proportion.[2]

There is no indication in Leonardo's Florentine drawings of the 1470s that he intended to pursue scientific studies of any kind in a structured manner, and the few rudimentary sketches of mechanisms among his early sheets show no knowledge beyond what was common for artists of the day. Around 1482 he moved to Milan and a draft of a letter successfully seeking employment at the Sforza court, undated but probably of the mid-1480s, makes clear that Leonardo's ambitions at that time lay in the practicalities of military engineering and architecture. It may have been his new status as a court artist that caused Leonardo to consider the theoretical basis of art. Many major artists of the Renaissance held an ambiguous position in society, as artisans who yet dealt directly with some of the most powerful and educated men of the day, and much of the writing on the arts in the fifteenth and sixteenth centuries aimed to demonstrate that painting and sculpture were elevated pursuits based on theoretical as well as practical knowledge. Leonardo expressly stated that this understanding of the physical world, and the consequent ability of the artist to invent new forms rather than simply replicating the visible, allowed painting to be classed among the Liberal Arts.[3]

Leonardo began to compile observations in a succession of notebooks during the last third of the 1480s, with the intention of preparing treatises both on painting and on the human body (though there was significant overlap between the two). The first outline of his proposed treatise on anatomy, written around 1489–90, includes all aspects of the conception and growth of the body, its form, proportions, constitution, nutrition, movements, senses and emotions. Some of the topics listed were never covered in any detail by Leonardo, and he must at first have felt daunted by the range of material that presented itself and the resistance to analysis of much of it. With a sense of relief, perhaps, he latched on to human proportion as an area that was finite, numerical and of direct relevance to the artist.

By 1489 Leonardo had attempted to locate the faculties of the brain by proportional means (CAT. 5), and his interest in the subject received a boost the following year when the peripatetic artist and engineer Francesco di Giorgio arrived in Milan. Francesco had translated Vitruvius into Italian and was working towards his own treatise on architecture and engineering, making a first attempt to put his material in order in the late 1480s. He was called to Milan in June 1490 to work on a scheme for the lantern of the cathedral, and in the same month was in Pavia with Leonardo to make recommendations on the construction of the cathedral there. Though Francesco di Giorgio stayed in Lombardy for no more than a few months, he and Leonardo must have become well acquainted, for Vitruvius was thereafter the basis for Leonardo's studies of human proportion, and there are many instances where he adopted Vitruvius' ratios without demur, most famously in his carefully finished drawing of a man within a square and a circle (FIG. 3).

Leonardo began his proportional researches by looking for parts of the body of equal length (FIG. 4) and then for fractional relationships, regardless of whether the parts compared were related anatomically. But Leonardo's researches throughout his life followed a familiar pattern, from a simple codification to ever more minute degrees of detail, and in the field of proportion he quickly recognised that any easily expressible system could not describe adequately the complexity of the human form. As soon as Leonardo began to measure the model, he found that many different fractions were necessary to fit the empirical data; and expressing measurements in terms of 4, 6, 7, 8, 9, 10, 12, 15, 16, 17, 18, 42, or 54 parts rather lost sight of the basis of proportional study, that the dimensions of the ideal body should be expressible in *simple* harmonic ratios.

FIG. 3
LEONARDO DA VINCI *(right)*
The proportions of the body according to Vitruvius, c.1490–92
Pen and ink with touches of wash, over stylus
34.4 × 24.5 cm (13⁹⁄₁₆ × 9⅝")
Venice, Galleria dell'Accademia, inv. 228

FIG. 4 *(below)*
LEONARDO DA VINCI
The male bust divided into lines of equal length, c.1490
Pen and ink, 14.5 × 13.2 cm (5¹¹⁄₁₆ × 5³⁄₁₆")
RL 12607

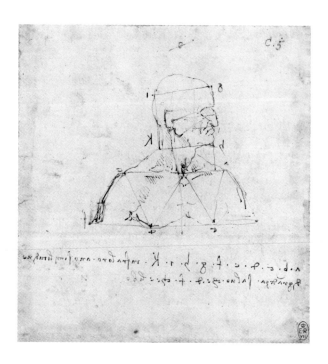

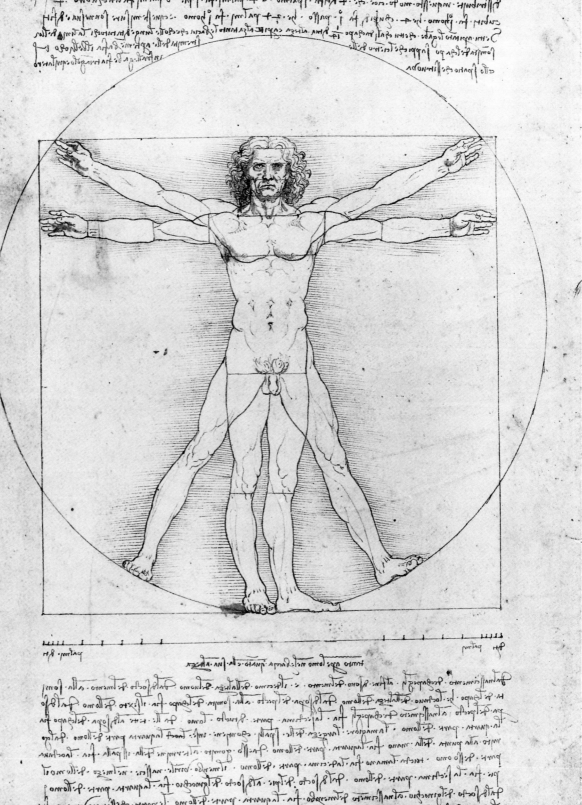

There is thus no final statement in Leonardo's notes of a theory of proportion,[4] though his drawings of this period were regarded by his successors as worthy of study and transmission. Two sixteenth-century manuscripts attempt to systematise Leonardo's theories, incidentally recording now-lost writings and drawings by the artist: the Codex Urbinas in the Vatican Library, a compendium of Leonardo's notes towards the treatise on painting by his pupil and heir Francesco Melzi, and the Codex Huygens in the Pierpont Morgan Library, New York, compiled by the painter Carlo Urbino around 1569. Both contain copies of Leonardo's proportional drawings and notes of around 1490, and we must suppose that his work on proportion was well known in artistic circles in Lombardy during the following century.[5]

What was probably a draft treatise by Leonardo, a 'praiseworthy book on painting and human movements', was mentioned by the mathematician Luca Pacioli in the preface to his own treatise *De divina proportione*, written in 1498 and published in 1509. Pacioli was one of the major propagators of mathematical knowledge in Italy in the late fifteenth century, having worked with Alberti in Rome and Piero della Francesca in Urbino in the 1470s, incorporating their writings into his own. He was in Milan from 1496 and helped Leonardo with the study of Euclid's *Elements*; in return, Leonardo provided the designs for the woodcuts of polyhedra that illustrate the first part of Pacioli's treatise. The consequent maturity of Leonardo's geometrical studies led him to abandon the attempt to codify a scheme of human proportion. He did not ignore proportions within the limbs (CAT. 13), or the dimensions of anatomical structures with respect to the basic units of foot or face (CAT. 14), regarding these quite reasonably as more useful than absolute measurements; but this was merely a small part of the description of the form and function of the body, rather than an end in itself. Proportion as a tool of investigation and reasoning became confined to its proper geometrically based fields of perspective, optics, and so on.

In addition to his studies of human proportion around 1490, Leonardo worked intensively on the proportions of the horse, prompted by a commission to sculpt a huge bronze equestrian monument to Francesco Sforza, the former Duke of Milan (see CAT. 7). Leonardo systematically surveyed the horse from orthogonal, or mutually perpendicular, viewpoints

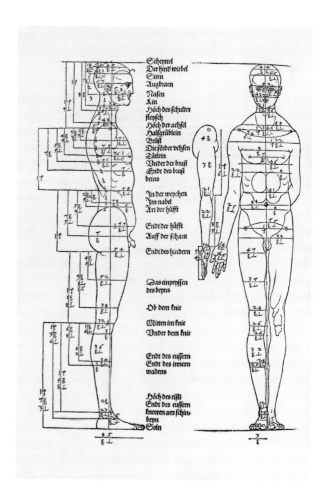

FIG. 5
ALBRECHT DÜRER (1471–1528)
The proportions of a tall thin man, from *Vier Bücher von menschlicher Proportion,* Nuremberg 1528
Woodcut, image 22.5 × 16.4 cm (8⅞ × 6⁷⁄₁₆″)

(CATS. 7–8), and several of his measured drawings are copied in the Codex Huygens, together with a larger number now lost. This material is coherent enough to support Giorgio Vasari's statement of 1568 that Leonardo had composed a treatise on the anatomy of the horse, already supposedly lost by Vasari's day.[6] Vasari's personal unfamiliarity with that treatise raises the possibility that it could have been identical with Leonardo's work on the proportions of the horse that Gian Paolo Lomazzo stated he was attempting to emulate in his own discussion of the subject, published in 1584.[7]

The equine studies were fundamentally different from Leonardo's contemporary studies of human proportion because the horse, unlike man, held no central place in the scheme of the universe, and could therefore not be expected to have any divinely harmonious relationships between its parts. To ascertain its form, abstract speculation was of no use: one simply had to measure the beast. The density of measurement in Leonardo's equine studies went far beyond what was of direct practical use to the artist, but these studies were methodologically in advance of his studies of the human form, for he was unencumbered by an urge to find correspondences and harmonic proportions.

Further, Leonardo distinguished between different breeds of horse, though he never waged a campaign of measurement of different human types in the manner of Albrecht Dürer's *Four Books on Human Proportion*, published in 1528 (FIG. 5). By the time Leonardo had abandoned the idea of a single canon of ideal proportion, he had also moved on from measurement as the key to description of the human body. After 1500, form, not measure, was the goal.

The French invasion of Milan in 1499 and the fall of his patron Ludovico Sforza caused Leonardo to leave the city after almost two decades there; travelling via Mantua and Venice he soon returned to Florence, the city of his youth. For a couple of years after this upheaval Leonardo seems not to have been able to settle his mind on any large-scale projects, either artistic or scientific. In April 1501 it was reported that Leonardo 'is entirely wrapped up in geometry and has no patience for painting', and that 'his mathematical experiments have made painting so distasteful to him that he cannot even bear to take up a brush.' These 'experiments' seem to have been paper exercises in pure mathematics and geometry, and when Leonardo returned to the study of the human form around 1504 he made no attempt to apply his mathematical knowledge to the body.

This next phase of Leonardo's studies of the body was in all likelihood prompted by the most prestigious commission of his career. Probably some time around the middle of 1503, Leonardo agreed to paint a huge mural of the *Battle of Anghiari* in the Palazzo della Signoria in Florence (see CATS. 47–8). In connection with this he made many drawings of male nudes, not studies directly for the composition, but surveys of the muscular body (CATS. 10–12). In those drawings there is no attempt to impose a system of proportion on the figure, nor to derive such a system from measurements taken from the model. He was concerned solely with the depiction of concrete form, and while there is undoubtedly an element of idealisation in the drawings, that ideal was aesthetic rather than mathematical.

Leonardo's inquiry into the physical actuality of the body reached its most profound level in the anatomical drawings that he made probably in the winter of 1510–11, in collaboration with the young professor of anatomy at the university of Pavia, Marcantonio della Torre (CATS. 13–14). Leonardo had then more access to human material than at any other stage of his career, and Marcantonio seems to have encouraged him to arrive at a working compromise between coverage and detail. Instead of searching for the anatomical forms that would fulfil certain preconceived functions, Leonardo first recorded as accurately as possible what he saw, analysing these structures as mechanical systems. No feature was redundant: every part had a purpose in a body perfectly made by the Creator, and this teleological concept underlies all of Leonardo's later anatomical notes.

During the course of his career Leonardo never relinquished the idea that the human body was divine, but the way in which he perceived that divinity changed fundamentally. His early studies embraced the concept that the human form was part of the divinely harmonious structure of the universe, to be laid bare by analysis of its proportions. His later work saw divinity in the functional perfection of the body's forms. Though such a definition may sound prosaic, Leonardo's ultimate apprehension of the infinite subtlety of creation was of far greater profundity than a hollow system of numbers.

1. Codex Urbinas f. 10r; Richter 1939, pp. 59f., no. 25.
2. For a solid introduction to proportion see Panofsky 1940, pp. 106–22, and 1955, with a good general bibliography in Berra 1993, p. 268 n.4. On Vitruvius in the Renaissance, see Zöllner 1987; on all aspects of Alberti, see Mantua 1994.
3. Codex Urbinas f. 15v; Richter 1939, p. 67, no. 30.
4. But see an over-rigorous attempt to systematise Leonardo's

proportional studies in Favaro 1917 and 1918.
5. See Panofsky 1940, Marinelli 1981 and Marinoni 1989. A good bibliography for the Codex Huygens is in Bambach Cappel 1994, p. 36 n. 54.
6. Vasari 1965, p. 264.
7. Lomazzo 1584, I, ch. XIX.

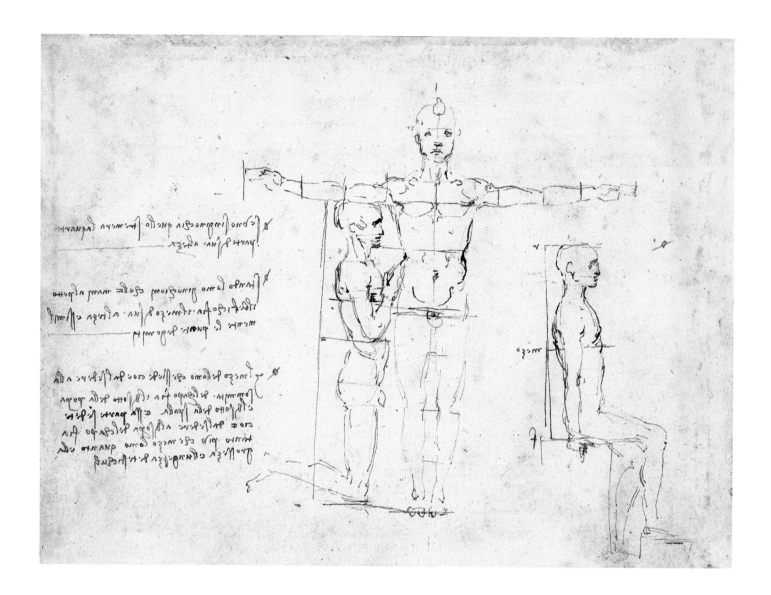

2

LEONARDO DA VINCI

The proportions of a standing, kneeling and sitting man, c.1490

Pen and ink, 16.1 × 21.8 cm (6⁵⁄₁₆ × 8⁹⁄₁₆″)
RL 19132 (Keele and Pedretti 1979, no. 27)

CATS. 2 and 3 are two of the series of sheets that form Leonardo's earliest and most sustained study of human proportion. All the drawings in this series are executed schematically in pen and ink with no under-drawing and are laid out unusually neatly, suggesting that Leonardo was making a 'fair copy' of rough notes compiled elsewhere.

The system of proportions in the central drawing follows that of Vitruvius. The height of a man was the basic unit, equal to the span of the outstretched arms. A quarter of the height was the cubit, and Leonardo marked off the cubits horizontally at the knee, the pubis and the centre of the chest, and vertically at the elbows. These divisions are also shown and explained on the drawing of the Vitruvian man in the Accademia in Venice (FIG. 3), along with the statements that the head is an eighth of the height, the length of the face and of the hand a tenth, the width of the palm one

twenty-fourth, and of the finger one ninety-sixth. Leonardo departed from Vitruvius only in stating that the length of the foot is a seventh of the height, whereas Vitruvius held it to be a sixth.

The notes to the left of the sheet explain the two subsidiary diagrams:

> If a man kneels he will diminish by a quarter part of his height.
> When a man is kneeling with his hands on his chest, the umbilicus is the middle of his height, and similarly the points of his elbows.

> The middle of a man who sits, that is, from the seat to the top of his head, is below the breast and below the shoulder. This sitting part, that is, from the seat to the top of the head, is as much more than half the man as is the size and length of the testicles.

3

Leonardo da Vinci
The proportions of the leg and foot, c.1490

Pen and ink, 40.4 × 28.1 cm (15⅞ × 11¹⁄₁₆″)
Numbered by Melzi *.16.*
RL 19136-9v (Keele and Pedretti 1979, no. 31v)

The simplicity of the Vitruvian precepts illustrated in CAT. 2 was abandoned when Leonardo began to measure the model. Here his specimen was an individual named twice as *Caravaggio* (after the town near Milan); the recto of the sheet and a companion sheet (RL 19134–5) repeat this name and also give the name of another model, *Trezzo*, again after a town near Milan.

The drawing is one of the earliest examples of overwhelming detail in Leonardo's scientific investigations. The notes beside the leg seen from the front read:

> *ac* is half a head, and is the same as *db*, and as the attachment of the five toes *ef*.
> *dk* diminishes a sixth in the leg at *gh*.
> *gh* is one-third of a head.
> *mn* increases by one-sixth from *ac* and is seven-twelfths of a head.
> *op* is one-tenth less than *dk* and is six-seventeenths of a head.
> *a* is in the middle between *q* and *b* and is one-quarter of a man.
> *r* is in the middle between *s* and *b*.
> The hollow on the outside of the knee at *r* is higher than the hollow on the inside at *a* by half the thickness of the leg at the foot.

And so on. The study of a pulley to the lower right, however, is accompanied by a note on basic mechanics:

> Five men against one thousand pounds in one hour; one man in five hours; a fifth of the force of one man in twenty-five hours. And in this way it always goes, he who lightens the work prolongs the time.

Within ten years Leonardo was to realise that such simple principles were a more productive application of his proportional studies than measuring the ankle, for instance, in terms of seventeenths of the head.

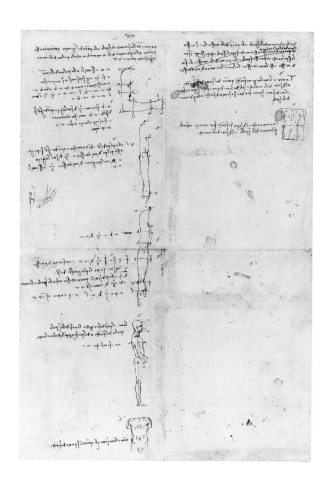

CAT. 3 (recto)

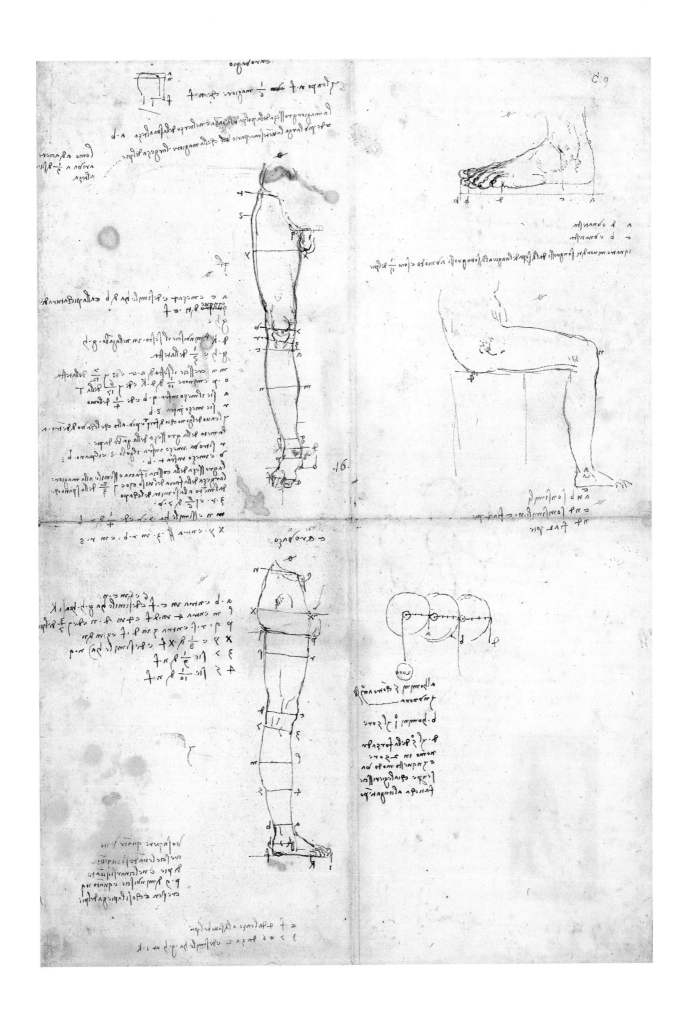

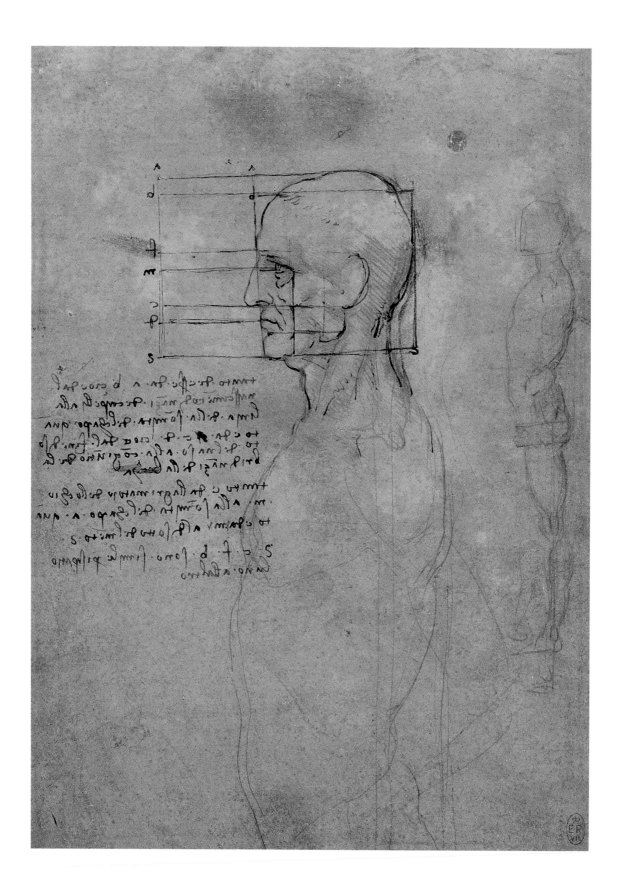

4

LEONARDO DA VINCI

The proportions of the head, and a
standing nude, c.1490

Metalpoint and pen and ink on blue prepared paper
21.3 × 15.3 cm (8⅜ × 6″)
RL 12601 (Keele and Pedretti 1979, no. 19)

The drawing is an example of Leonardo's early attempts
to find correspondences of length between parts of the
body, without the use of fractions. Intriguingly, these
proportions are here applied not to the neutral, youthful profile, but to the older warrior type, who might be
thought to manifest the distortions of the ageing
process.

> It is as far from *a* to *b*, that is, from the start of
> the hair at the front to the line of the top of the
> head, as it is from *c* to *d*, that is, from the lower
> end of the nose to the junction of the lips at the
> front of the mouth.

> It is as far from the tearduct of the eye *m* to
> the top of the head *a*, as it is from *m* to below
> the chin *s*.

> *s c f b* are equal to one another as to distance.

Leonardo thus distinguished between two different
basic units: the height of the head (*as*), and the face
measured from chin to hairline (*bs*). This definition of
a unit of the face may seem odd, given the variability
of the hairline between individuals, but was common
in proportional studies of the period (although confus-
ingly the unit of the face was itself sometimes termed
a *testa* or head).

Leonardo inked over the metalpoint outlines to
clarify the diagram, adjusting the line of the back of
the cranium to make the depth of the head (from the
line touching brow, lips and chin) equal to the height
of the face. He placed the eye at the mid-point of the
head and divided the face into three equal sections,
from the base of the chin to the base of the nose,
thence to the brow, and thence to the hairline. These
divisions were explored further on a sheet in Venice
(FIG. 6), where the intervals were treated explicitly as
fractions of the head or face.[1]

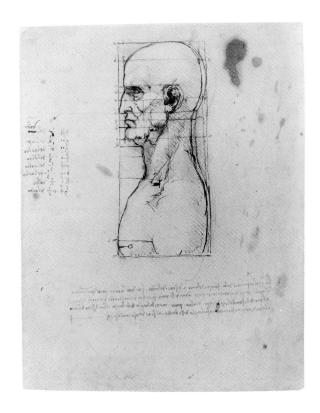

FIG. 6
LEONARDO DA VINCI
The proportions of the head, c.1490
Pen and ink over black chalk, 28.0 × 22.2 cm (11 × 8¾″)
Venice, Galleria dell'Accademia, inv. 236v

1.   Other related drawings are in the Biblioteca Reale,
     Turin (inv. 15574/6), and in Paris MS A, f. 63r; see
     Venice 1992, pp. 224–7.

5

LEONARDO DA VINCI
The skull sectioned, 1489

Black chalk and stylus underdrawing, pen and ink
18.8 × 13.4 cm (7⅜ × 5¼″)
RL 19057 (Keele and Pedretti 1979, no. 43)

Most of Leonardo's early anatomical studies, around 1490, were based on traditional beliefs and, to a lesser degree, the dissection of animal material. He had little access to human material, and that little seems to have been entirely skeletal. Although Leonardo wrote out a scheme for his intended treatise on anatomy, there is no programme evident in the surviving miscellaneous drawings of this period, which are often diagrammatic in character and full of errors.

Quite exceptional, therefore, is a series of studies of the human skull from the so-called Anatomical Manuscript B, one of which (RL 19059r) is dated 2 April 1489, the first firm date for Leonardo's anatomical work. The studies were drawn from specimens that he had sectioned in a highly intelligent and innovative fashion to display the internal structure of the cranium in relation to its external features. Leonardo depicted several structures for the first time in the history of anatomical illustration, such as the frontal and sphenoidal sinuses and the pituitary fossa; the cervical vertebrae are very schematically drawn, however, and it is likely that Leonardo had only a skull and jaw from which to work.

But structural accuracy was not in itself the purpose of the drawing. Leonardo wished to establish the site of the *senso comune*, where all the sensory nerves supposedly converged, a point that he located just behind the optic foramina, at the pole of the axial lines in the upper drawing.

The first note explains the lower drawing:

Where the line *am* intersects the line *cb*, there is the meeting of all the senses, and where the line *rn* intersects the line *hf*, there is the fulcrum of the cranium, at one third from the base of the head; and so *cb* is halfway.

While the line *cb* does indeed bisect the height of the head, the line *hf* does not lie at one-third as stated. Leonardo's ongoing belief that the universe (and thus man) should be harmoniously constructed meant that he was willing to override his own experience – even data as basic as measurement – in order to demonstrate the supposedly simple proportions of the skull.

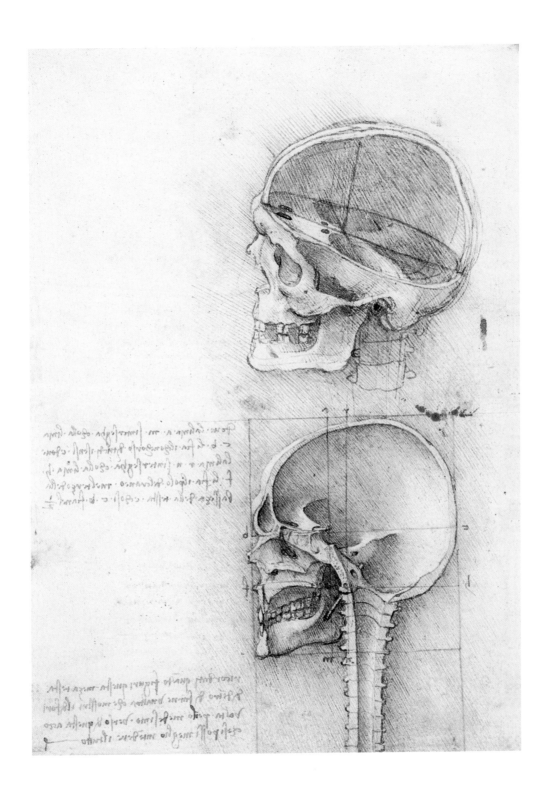

6

Leonardo da Vinci
A horse in left profile, the body divided by lines, c.1480

Scratchy black chalk underdrawing, pen and ink
29.7 × 28.9 cm (11¹¹⁄₁₆ × 11⅜″), upper left corner
and a rectangle at upper right cut away
Numbered by Melzi 42
RL 12318 (Pedretti 1987, no. 88)

The style of the drawing, with vigorous, crudely drawn outlines and small areas of scribbled hatching, is that of Leonardo's first Florentine period, and the physical type of the horse, with a small, unclassical head, loose mane and forward-pointing ears, is typical of Leonardo's early drawings, such as the studies for the unfinished *Adoration of the Magi* of 1481.

Although apparently confident and imposing, the drawing is uncertain in purpose, and the absence of annotations suggests that Leonardo simply sketched a horse and drew lines between salient points, without beginning to measure a live animal. He may have been prompted to make such a study, albeit half-heartedly, in emulation of the researches of his former associate and possible master Andrea del Verrocchio, whose last great work was his bronze equestrian monument to Bartolomeo Colleoni (Venice, Campo di SS Giovanni e Paolo).

The Colleoni monument was commissioned in April 1480 on the basis of a full-size model, and Verrocchio had presumably studied equine dimensions in the late 1470s. A drawing in the Metropolitan Museum of Art, New York (FIG. 7), attributed to Verrocchio, depicts a horse standing in left profile with lines drawn between points of the body, as here, and measurements written over the lines.[1] Leonardo was documented still living in Verrocchio's house in 1476, and it is reasonable to suppose that they remained intimate for the remainder of their time in Florence, and that Leonardo would have been familiar with the preparatory work on the Colleoni monument. The unit of measurement in Verrocchio's study is the head divided into sixteenths, the same system that Leonardo was to use when he began to measure horses himself a decade later.

---

1. Bean 1982, no. 270; Scaglia 1982. In the Galleria Corsini, Rome (inv. 127615) is a double-sided sheet of studies of horses, also by Verrocchio, in more natural poses with some measurements indicated; repr. Pedretti 1987, p. 148.

FIG. 7
Attributed to Andrea del Verrocchio (c.1435–88)
The dimensions of a horse, c.1475–80
Pen and ink, over a little black chalk
24.9 × 29.8 cm (9¹³⁄₁₆ × 11¾″)
New York, Metropolitan Museum of Art, inv. 19.76.5

7

LEONARDO DA VINCI
A horse in left profile, with measurements, c.1490

Metalpoint on blue prepared paper, the outlines
of the main figure incised; sharply folded in two,
the upper half damaged, 32.4 × 23.7 cm (12¼ × 9⁵⁄₁₆″)
Inscribed by a sixteenth-century hand, upper right,
de Lionardo
RL 12319 (Pedretti 1987, no. 89)

CAT. 7 is one of a series of drawings in metalpoint on
blue paper that study the dimensions and surface modelling of the horse from the front and side, in preparation for an equestrian monument to Francesco Sforza
(1401–66). Sometime during the 1480s Francesco's son
Ludovico commissioned Leonardo to execute the
monument, but in 1489 the Florentine ambassador in
Milan wrote to Lorenzo de' Medici that Ludovico
requested the names of other artists who might be
more suited to the project, as he was not confident
that Leonardo understood how to complete the work.
Evidently Leonardo overcame the Duke's doubts, for
on 23 April 1490 he recorded, 'I recommenced the
horse.' Over the next few years he prepared a full-size
clay model from which a sectional mould was made,
but in November 1494 the French invasion of Italy
caused Ludovico Sforza to send the bronze intended
for the monument to his father-in-law Ercole d'Este,
Duke of Ferrara, to be made into cannon, and work
seems never to have resumed on the project.

Leonardo's note above the main drawing, *gianecto
grosso di messer galeazo*, records that the horse was a
large jennet (a breed of Spanish riding horse) belonging to Galeazzo Sanseverino, the Captain-General of
the Milanese army. Measuring a live horse must have
been slow work, and it is probable that Leonardo
annotated the surviving drawings on the basis of
measurements dictated to (or by) an assistant. The

larger distances were presumably measured with a
tape; the thicknesses of the legs were obtained with
caliper compasses, four of which Leonardo drew in a
notebook compiled at the end of the 1480s.[1]

Leonardo used as his unit the head (measured from
the tip of the muzzle to the base of the ears) divided
into sixteenths, the same system as used in the studies
of horses attributed to Verrocchio (FIG. 7). Leonardo
expressed further subdivisions of these sixteenths
either as fractions (halves, thirds and quarters of a sixteenth, as seen here) or in terms of a unit itself one-
sixteenth of a sixteenth, and thus 1/256 of a head. This
tiny unit, less than 2 mm, is comparable to Alberti's
minutum, 1/600 the height of man, or Dürer's *Trümlein*,
1/1800 of a man or 1 mm.

The sheet was folded in two before Leonardo
began work on it, and the drawings in the two halves of
the sheet are upside down with respect to one another.
At some point in its history the folded drawing became
stuck to some other surface, probably by damp, and
subsequently lost large patches of the blue preparation
in the upper half of the sheet, taking the metalpoint of
Leonardo's drawings with it. The sheet was rubbed
with red chalk on the verso, and the outlines of the
principal study incised with a sharp stylus to trace it on
to another sheet, though it is not found copied in the
pages of the Codex Huygens; oddly, only the marginal
studies here are reproduced in that manuscript.

1.   Paris MS B, ff. 52v, 57v, 58v.

8

LEONARDO DA VINCI
A horse's left foreleg, with measurements,
*c.*1490–92

Charcoal(?) underdrawing, pen and ink
25.0 × 18.7 cm (9^{13}⁄$_{16}$ × 7⅜″)
Numbered by Melzi *.41.*
RL 12294 (Pedretti 1987, no. 94)

Most of Leonardo's measured drawings of horses show the animal standing with all legs straight, but several details study the dimensions of the raised left foreleg. This reflects the intended final form of the Sforza monument, which is seen in exactly this pose in a sketch of the frame for the transport of the clay model, where the hoof rests on a vase.[1] In the note below the drawing Leonardo reminds himself to 'make this the same within [i.e. from the other side of the leg] with the measurement of the whole shoulder.'

Leonardo's surveys of horses were drawn freehand and the measurements added, rather than being constructed from these measurements. Thus Leonardo never had to confront the real problems that would face an artist attempting to construct a horse (whether drawn, painted or sculpted) from a plethora of dimensions. If the measured drawings were used at all during Leonardo's preparations for the Sforza monument, it is more likely that they served as a check (with a scaling factor) on the dimensions of the clay model. The statue was to be about three times life-size, and errors of proportion would have been difficult to apprehend when working close to the model.

The drawing is labelled *Cicilano dj meser galeazo*, identifying the model as a Sicilian belonging to Galeazzo Sanseverino (see CAT. 7), the subject of more of Leonardo's drawings than any other horse. In addition to the copy of the present sheet on folio 77 of the Codex Huygens, that manuscript also contains copies of lost drawings of the Sicilian on folios 71 (from above), 72 (from the front), 73 (from behind), 80 (the hindquarters), and 84 and 86 (in right profile).

1.   Codex Atlanticus, f. 216v-a; Milan 1998–9b, no. 6.

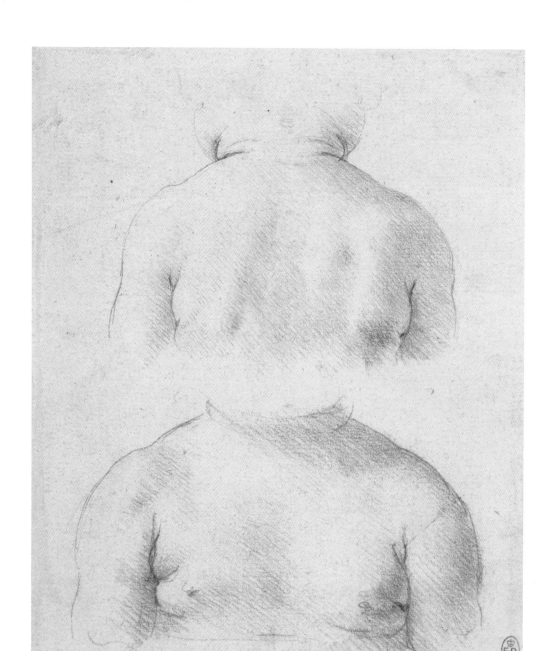

9

LEONARDO DA VINCI
The bust of a child from front and back, c.1495

Red chalk, 16.5 × 13.5 cm (6½ × 5⁵⁄₁₆″)
RL 12567

Leonardo's first outline for his treatise on anatomy, drafted around 1490, included a reminder to record 'which are the members which, after the child is born, grow more than the others, and determine the measurements of a child of one year.'[1] There is, however, no indication in Leonardo's surviving proportional drawings that he attempted to codify the dimensions of the child; the variable growth rates of the different parts, and from child to child, would have rendered this impractical. This drawing seems therefore to be a purely visual survey of the soft contours of a thriving infant, without any attempt to analyse its proportions. The rather insecure outlines and dry hatching are typical of Leonardo's early drawings in red chalk, around the middle of the 1490s. It may well be associated with CAT. 15, also in red chalk, showing an infant in left profile: in each drawing there is an identical roll of puppy-fat at the child's neck and the bust is terminated below at the same level, and they may therefore be connected in some way with a sculpted bust.

It is impossible to generalise about the drawing habits of Renaissance sculptors, other than that they seem to have drawn little, presumably preferring to 'sketch' their ideas as small models in clay or wax; but sculptors who were also painters, such as Leonardo, may well have prepared their three-dimensional pieces in a different manner from those who practised sculpture alone. Leonardo had also been involved in architectural projects, with an emphasis on plan and elevation, and he had measured man and horse from orthogonal viewpoints around 1490 (CATS. 2–8). Within continuous space Leonardo would have had a heightened awareness of the geometrical convention of orthogonals, and this must have affected the way in which he perceived (and conceived) solid form.

1. RL 19037v; Richter 1939, no. 797.

10

LEONARDO DA VINCI

*A nude man from the front, and
a partial study of the left leg, c.1504–6*

Red chalk on red prepared paper
22.5 × 16.6 cm (8⅞ × 6⁹⁄₁₆″)
Numbered by Melzi .69.
RL 12593 (Keele and Pedretti 1979, no. 85)

11

LEONARDO DA VINCI

A nude man from the front, c.1504–6

Red chalk and pen and ink on red prepared paper
23.6 × 14.6 cm (9⁵⁄₁₆ × 5¾″)
Numbered by Melzi 61.
RL 12594 (Keele and Pedretti 1979, no. 86)

12

LEONARDO DA VINCI

A nude man from behind, c.1504–6

Red chalk, 27.0 × 16.0 cm (10⅝ × 6⁵⁄₁₆″)
RL 12596 (Keele and Pedretti 1979, no. 84)
Exhibited in London only

Around the time of his work towards the great mural of the *Battle of Anghiari* (see CATS. 47–48), Leonardo made many studies of male nudes, both in action and, as here, at rest. In these there was no attempt either to derive a system of proportions or to impose such a system on the figures. Leonardo had effectively abandoned the belief in measurement as the key to the human form that had motivated his researches of fifteen years before; while there are occasional references to measurements in Leonardo's later anatomical drawings (CATS. 13–14), these are entirely incidental. In the years after 1500 it was an empirical understanding of the physical reality of the body that most interested Leonardo.

The nude studies were not directly preparatory for the *Battle of Anghiari*, but constituted background research on the human form. Here the model spread his legs equally to balance his weight distribution, and (in CATS. 10–11) supported his arms by holding sticks so as to put no strain on the shoulder muscles. While it was important for expressive purposes to know how to draw the muscles in tension, it was just as important to know how to draw them when relaxed:

> You should not make all the muscles of your figures conspicuous; even if they are shown in the correct place they should not be made too evident, unless the limbs to which they belong are engaged in the exertion of great force or labour; and the limbs that are not under strain should have no such display of musculature. If you do otherwise you will have produced a sack of nuts rather than a human figure.[1]

The drawings were studies in contour as well as surface modelling, and Leonardo repeatedly went over the outlines of CAT. 10 with the wetted tip of the chalk, and of CAT. 11 with pen and ink. This may have been made necessary by the choice of red prepared paper for red chalk drawings, which limited the tonal range available; CAT. 12, on white paper, had no need of such strengthening, and the light strokes of the chalk outlines retain the freshness of the life study. The model for that drawing may be identified by a cut inscription at top left, *franc sinisstre sonat*[…], as a musician (*sonatore*) named Francesco Sinistre; though this is not a likely surname, it may have indicated a left-handed player.

CAT. 11 seems to have enjoyed some celebrity in later sixteenth-century Milan. It was reproduced on the title page of *Rabisch dra Academiglia dor Compa Zavargna, Nabad dra Vall d'Bregn* (1589), a compendium of mock-serious writings in a contrived dialect by Gian Paolo Lomazzo (*Compa Zavargna*), in his capacity as abbot (*Nabad*) of the Accademia del Val di Blenio.[2] A copy of CAT. 11 at Windsor (RL 12595), with the addition of a beard, may indeed be by Lomazzo.[3]

1. Madrid MS II, f. 128r.
2. See Berra 1993; Lugano 1998, no. 29.
3. Clark and Pedretti 1968–9, I, p. 120.

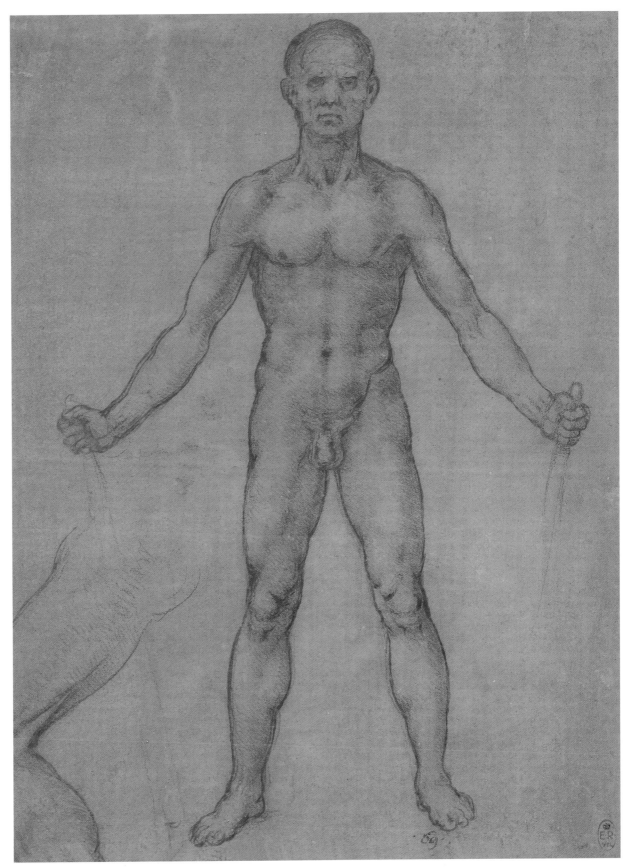

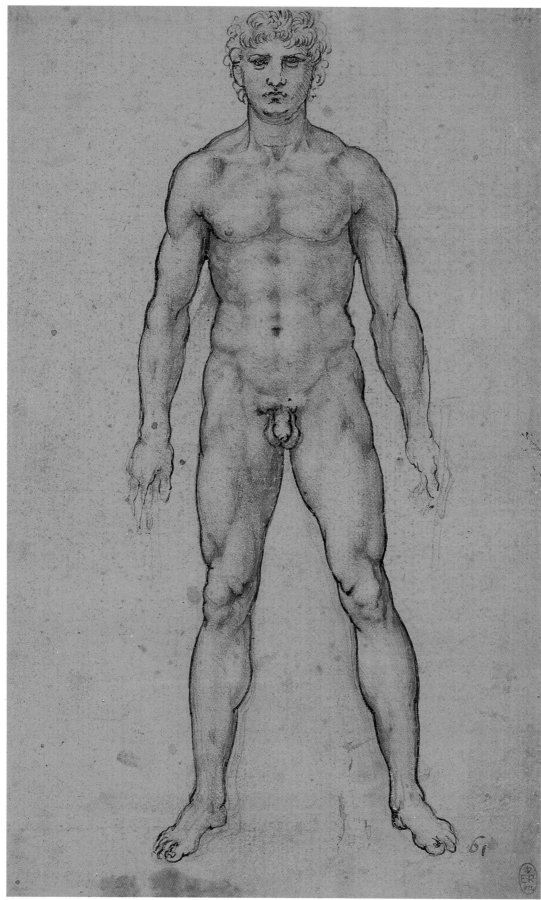

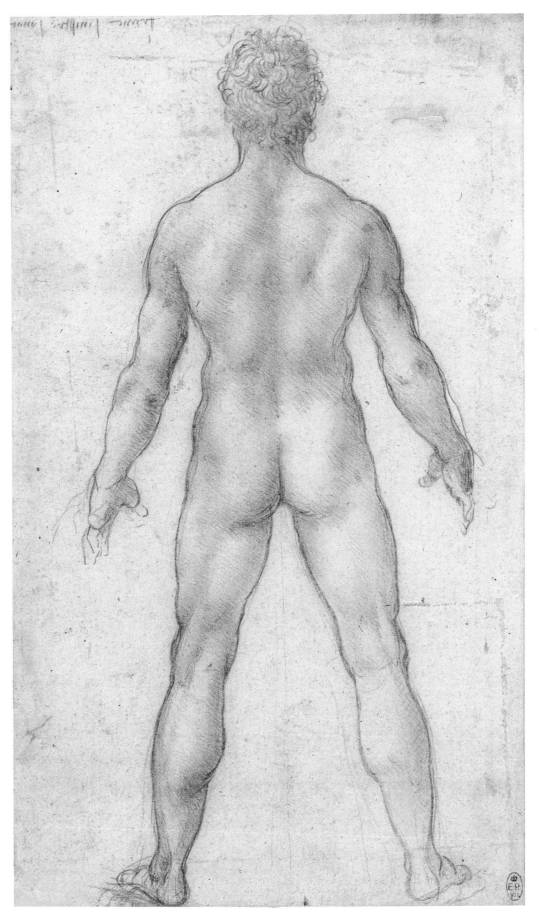

13

LEONARDO DA VINCI
The bones of the arm, c.1510–11

Pen and ink with wash, over traces of black chalk
29.3 × 20.1 cm (11⁹⁄₁₆ × 7¹⁵⁄₁₆″)
RL 19000v (Keele and Pedretti 1979, no. 135v)

CATS. 13 and 14 formed part of the so-called Anatomical
Manuscript A, a series of sheets compiled by Leonardo
probably in collaboration with Marcantonio della
Torre at the medical school of Pavia in the winter of
1510–11. This was the period of Leonardo's greatest
achievements as an artist-anatomist, and his beautiful
and lucid drawings of the mechanics of bones and
muscles have seldom, if ever, been bettered in the succeeding five centuries.

The present sheet examines the rotation (supina-
tion and pronation) of the forearm, showing the role
of the biceps, its double origin (hence its name, meaning 'two headed') and its point of insertion on the
radius. Leonardo noted by the top drawing that 'The
hand from *f* to *a* is six-sevenths of the bone *ab* [radius]'
and 'The bones *ab* are five-sevenths of the length of
the bone *bc* [humerus], the arm being extended with
the palm turned towards the sky.' The attitude of the
palm was significant because, as Leonardo noted:

> the arm, which has two bones [radius and ulna]
> between the hand and the elbow, will be
> somewhat shorter when the palm of the hand
> faces the ground [pronation] than when it faces
> the sky, when a man stands with his arm
> extended. And this happens because the two
> bones … become crossed.

The reason for this is illustrated by the geometrical diagram in the right margin with the note 'that line loses
depth the more obliquely it is placed.' While Leonardo
had not abandoned proportional considerations alto-
gether, here he confined his statements to the perfectly
proper matter of the ratio of upper arm to lower arm
to hand, with a qualification based on a subtle piece of
anatomical and geometrical understanding.

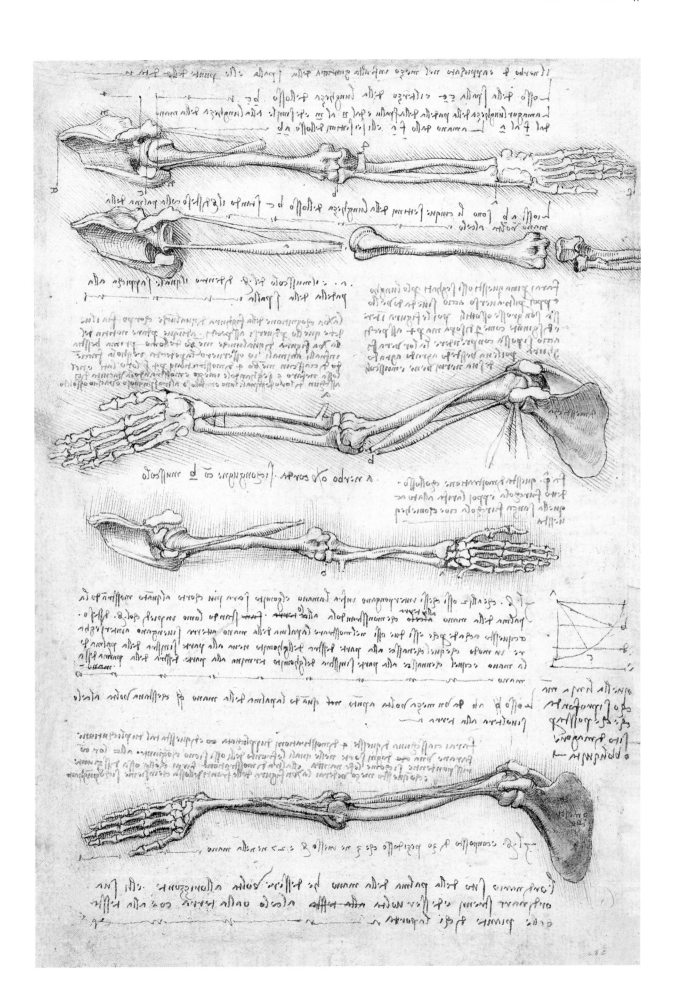

14

LEONARDO DA VINCI
The skeleton, c.1510–11

Pen and ink with wash, over traces of black chalk
28.8 × 20.0 cm (11⁵⁄₁₆ × 7⁷⁄₈″)
RL 19012r (Keele and Pedretti 1979, no. 142r)

This is Leonardo's most complete study of the human skeleton. The series of orthogonal elevations show the thorax from back, right side and front, the pelvis and legs from front and left side, and a detail shows the attachment of the patella.

The sheet is a particularly clear example of Leonardo's method of compiling much of Anatomical MS A. The page was first headed 'What are the parts of man where the flesh does not ever increase through any fatness, and what are those places where the flesh increases more than anywhere else.' But the mass of information that Leonardo gained during his campaign of dissection in the winter of 1510–11 supplanted the topics that he had intended to cover, for the drawings of the skeleton that fill the page are quite unrelated to that heading; in fact, unlike Dürer (FIG. 5, p. 24), Leonardo seems never to have analysed different physical types (tall and thin, short and fat), though he did propose the subject on several occasions.

Many of the notes in Anatomical MS A relate to methods of representation. Leonardo wished to display his new-found knowledge as clearly as possible, and he repeatedly reminded himself to draw each structure at each stage of dissection, often from three or more orthogonal viewpoints: 'You will make the first demonstration of the ribs in three figures without the scapula, and then three others with the scapula'; 'Before you put in place the bone to the arm *m* [humerus] draw the opposite face of the shoulder which receives it, that is, the concavity of the scapula; and do the same with every joint'; 'Make these two scapulae to be seen thus situated from above, below, from opposite sides, behind, in front.'

Only one of the notes on this page describes the dimensions of the thorax, with reference to the drawing at upper right:

> From the first rib *a* to the fourth below *b* is equal to the scapula of the shoulder *cd*; and is equal to the hand, and to the foot from its fulcrum to the point of the foot, and each is equal to the face.

This echo of Leonardo's pursuit of equivalences of twenty years before is exceptional in the Anatomical MS A, and was overwhelmed by the mass of profoundly original observations about the structure and mechanisms of the body.

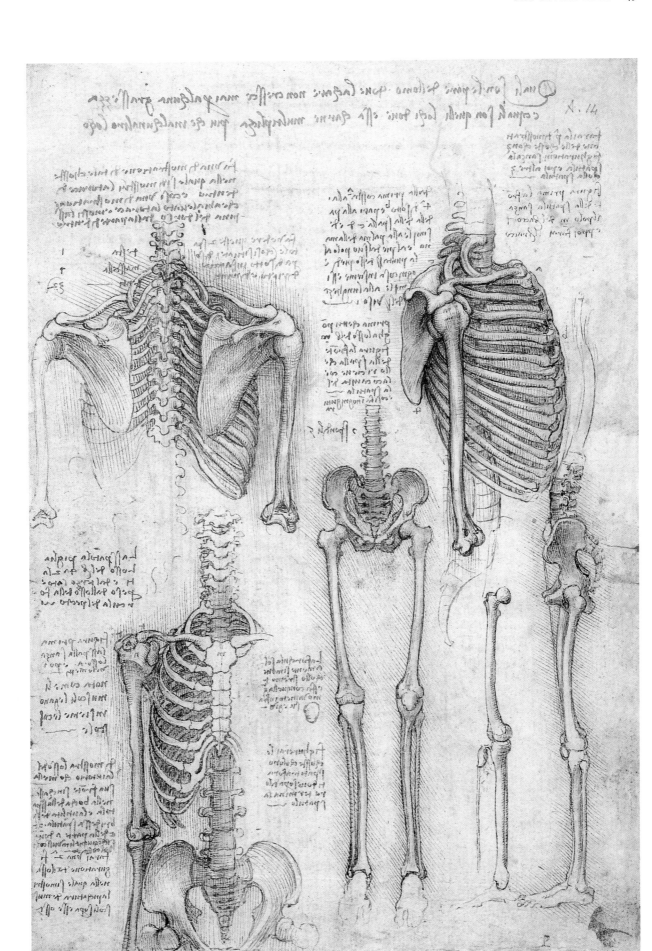

IDEAL TYPES

Certain male facial types recur in Leonardo's art throughout his career. During his early twenties, in the workshop of the Florentine sculptor and painter Andrea del Verrocchio, he assimilated the two distinct types that are found repeatedly in Verrocchio's work – a youth with a straight nose, lightly rounded chin and open expression, and a mature man with an aquiline nose, prominent chin and beetling brow. Several bust-length reliefs in profile of two warriors with these features (often identified as Darius and Alexander, or Hannibal and Scipio) survive in a range of media from Verrocchio's workshop and beyond (FIG. 8), and it is clear that they were conceived as a pair. The same two types are seen among the bystanders in Verrocchio's silver relief of the *Beheading of the Baptist* (Florence, Museo dell'Opera del Duomo), and may be recognised in other single works by Verrocchio – the youth in the bronze *David* (Florence, Museo Nazionale del Bargello), the aged warrior in the equestrian figure of Bartolomeo Colleoni.[1]

FIG. 8
Circle of ANDREA DEL VERROCCHIO
*A bust of a warrior ('Alexander'), c.*1470–80
Marble, 55.9 × 36.7 cm (22 × 14⁷⁄₁₆")
Washington, National Gallery of Art, Gift of
Therese K. Straus

FIG. 9
LEONARDO DA VINCI
*A bust of a warrior, c.*1475–80
Metalpoint on buff prepared paper
28.7 × 21.2 cm (11⁵⁄₁₆ × 8³⁄₈")
London, British Museum, 1895-9-15-474

Although every artist in Florence in the 1470s would have known these two types well – Verrocchio ran one of the largest studios in the city, and several leading artists of the next generation worked there for a period – it was Leonardo who absorbed them into his own vision most readily, and with their range of variants they can be found throughout his work. Leonardo's most impressive early use of the older type, a drawing of a warrior in profile in the British Museum (FIG. 9), may even have been a copy of a Verrocchiesque relief, though this motif of a warrior in fantastic armour was popular throughout Italian art of the later Quattrocento. Both the 'warrior' and youthful types occur on one of Leonardo's earliest surviving sheets, with a profile study for the angel in the *Annunciation* on one side and the rugged profile of an older man on the other.[2] They lie at either end of the spectrum explored in CAT. 1, and Leonardo used them

repeatedly in the major painting of his first Florentine period, the *Adoration of the Magi* of 1481, now in the Uffizi, Florence. A dated drawing of 1478 places the two profiles opposite each other,[3] and in a sheet of the 1490s the youth gazes implacably at an aged, bald, toothless version of the mature man (FIG. 10). This juxtaposition of two contrasting motifs (of any kind) to emphasise the qualities of each was a standard device of classical rhetoric, and was adapted to become a familiar tool of the visual arts during the Renaissance.[4]

The genre of the independent imaginary head was already well established in Italian art, and its most popular manifestation, especially in northern Italy, was the head in the antique manner. It is misleading to describe such heads as intrinsically 'Leonardesque', for although his later eminence gave a certain authority to the classical profiles, Leonardo was following rather than initiating the tradition. These heads were derived from ancient coins and medals, the most plentiful and affordable form of antique art and of particular interest in a city such as Milan that was not endowed with major pieces of antique sculpture.[5] The classical head in profile thus became a standard decorative motif in Lombardy and beyond, where a number of distinct types based on the coinage of specific emperors can be found adorning armour, the borders of manuscripts, and especially buildings (FIGS. 11, 12), most vibrantly the tondi by Giovanni Antonio Amadeo at the Certosa di Pavia, ten miles south of Milan (1474–80).[6] The heads were mostly used without any overt connotations: while the artist and patron may have been aware whether the Nero or Hadrian, Galba or Vespasian type was being deployed, the choice carried no meaning.

Both of Leonardo's standard types, the youth and the old man, thus became noticeably more classical after his move to Milan. During the 1490s Leonardo's youths became more fleshy and weaker in the chin, approaching the type of the Emperor Nero.[7] The youths' hair changed from shoulder-length, straight at the crown and waving towards the ends, to a head of curls. Decoratively curled hair was a feature of Roman busts of the Hadrianic period,[8] but Leonardo's fascination with this type of hair may have had a more personal origin. In 1490 the 10-year-old Gian Giacomo Caprotti, known as Salaì, entered Leonardo's studio as an assistant, and was to stay with him until the artist's death twenty-nine years later. Gian Paolo Lomazzo wrote explicitly of the homosexual nature of the relationship between Leonardo and Salaì,[9] and Giorgio

Vasari described Salaì as 'a very attractive youth of unusual grace and looks, with very beautiful hair which he wore curled in ringlets and which delighted his master.'[10] While the youthful profiles cannot be portraits of Salaì in a literal sense, as was once thought – they do not change over the long period that he was with Leonardo – it does seem that the artist's ideal of male beauty was transformed by his relationship with the maturing boy, and that his repeated drawing of the youthful head, merging elements of Salaì's features with those of Nero, were attempts to hone the precise proportions that constituted Leonardo's ideal.[11]

Leonardo's older warrior type was more variable, and its personal meaning more equivocal; he cannot be considered beautiful in the same sense as the youth, though at his most virile he has a certain grandeur. Having been rather rustic in Florence, this type soon approximated to the type of Galba, the most martial of the emperors. These heads may be fierce in aspect, but they are not angry – they are essentially expressionless, in the sense that the faces do not respond to some inner emotion but are fixed in this form, either by nature or by a lifetime's habit. Very few of Leonardo's independent drawings of heads manifest any interest in conveying emotion (see 'Expression', CATS. 47–50).

Leonardo frequently exaggerated the features of the warrior to produce, not an even more virile figure, but a pathetic old man. The corners of the firmly set mouth were turned further down, the aquiline nose hooked, the clenched jaw stuck out and the lips sucked in over missing teeth. Leonardo's earlier depictions of

as the soul was responsible both for shaping the body and for guiding the hand of the artist, there was a tendency for artists to depict themselves, a phenomenon known as automimesis. This was not a consequence of egotism or narcissism, but a fundamental urge of the judgement to produce things that resemble itself. More generally, the particularities of his soul led the artist to develop and rely upon a few set types. Leonardo cautioned against this repeatedly in his notes, insisting on the need to study nature in all its variety, but as seen in the following section it is striking how far he was from following his own advice. Indeed it is possible that Leonard's awareness of the idea of automimesis made him more accepting of his lifelong attachment to these types, for his drawings were personal expressions, not intended to be seen and judged.[12]

In the last decade or so of his life Leonardo revived the genre of the carefully finished independent head study, familiar from the Florence of his youth. Most of the drawings in the following section have no preparatory purpose and illustrate nothing other than a certain facial type; they are examples of Leonardo's tendency late in his career to produce drawings that have no overt function but are simply exercises in form for his own satisfaction, and may be regarded as explorations of Leonardo's perception of his own character or projections of his psyche. At this point of deep introspection it becomes impossible to separate the ideal from the grotesque, and the two categories merge in images that are both noble and pathetic (CATS. 24–5).

FIG. 13
LEONARDO DA VINCI
*An old man seated in right profile, c.*1508–10
Pen and ink, area shown 15.2 × 10.8 cm (6 × 4¼″)
RL 12579 (detail)

1.   See especially Chastel 1978.
2.   Uffizi 449-E; Popham 1946, no. 130A.
3.   Uffizi 446-E; Popham 1946, no. 127; Florence 1992, no. 6.6.
4.   See Moffitt 1994, and CAT. 27.
5.   Weiss 1968.
6.   See especially Agosti 1990, pp. 47–102; Schofield 1997.
7.   Gombrich 1976, p. 70; Cunnally 1988; Cunnally 1993.
8.   Marani 2000, pp. 251–9.
9.   London, British Library, MS Add. 12196ff. 51v–67r; see Pedretti 1991a, p. 36.
10. Vasari 1965, p. 265.
11. On Salaì see Shell and Sironi 1991 and 1992. Gould (1975, p. 125) speculated that *St John the Baptist* in the Louvre, Paris, was a likeness of Salaì, and that in that painting Leonardo was 'working off his feelings against the race of half-men [i.e. homosexuals] with whom his proclivities forced him to associate.'
12. On automimesis see Gombrich 1976, p. 70; Kemp 1976; Vertova 1992; Zöllner 1992.

old men tend to be rather comic; as he himself aged, they assume a greater gravitas (FIG. 13), and just as the youthful profile was thought to be a portrait of Salaì, so the old man has been regarded as a self-portrait of Leonardo. Again, this cannot be literally true, as the gnarled warrior occurs throughout Leonardo's life, and the few reliable images of Leonardo show that he retained a fine, even delicate profile into old age (CAT. 46). But by idealising his young companion as the Nero type, Leonardo may have come to regard its pendant, the aged warrior, as at some level a self-image.

It was a commonly accepted neoplatonic idea that,

15

LEONARDO DA VINCI
The bust of a child in left profile
*c.*1495

Red chalk
10.0 × 10.0 cm ($3^{15}/_{16}$ × $3^{15}/_{16}$")
Numbered by Melzi *.3*.
RL 12519

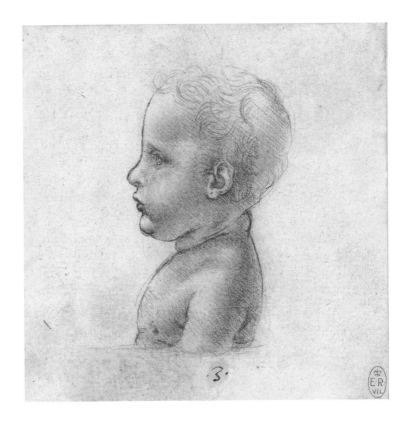

The profile was once thought to be a study for the *Virgin of the Rocks*, for it strongly resembles the Child in the later version of that painting (London, National Gallery). The dry red-chalk style of the drawing would be consistent with a date in the mid-1490s, but this was a common profile for representations of an infant, with a high forehead, slightly upturned nose, protruding upper lip and tightly rounded chin; the same combination is seen in CAT. 1, a drawing of some fifteen years earlier. Infants resemble each other more closely than do adults, and artists of the Renaissance usually reproduced a standard type for the Christ Child (for instance), rather than making a fresh study from the life in each case. Even on the rare occasions that individual children were portrayed, they were so generalised to this type as to be almost meaningless as portraits in the normal sense.[1]

CAT. 15 is thus unusual in being, apparently, drawn from the life, and this may have been prompted by its function. While Leonardo was content to reproduce the usual form of an infant's profile, the modelling of the flesh in the round seems to have been the focus of both this study and of CAT. 9, with which it is surely associated. This is suggestive not of a study for a painting but rather for a three-dimensional bust. No such bust by Leonardo has been identified – indeed, there is no work of sculpture that is generally accepted as being by the artist – but Lomazzo described a terracotta bust of a Christ Child in his own collection, supposedly by Leonardo himself, 'in which the simplicity and purity of the child appears with an added touch that denotes wisdom, intellect and majesty, and the countenance, while retaining the character of a tender child, seems to express the wisdom of old age.'[2] This classical topos of *puer et senex*, or boy and old man – a mental maturity (moral or wise, rather than intellectual) precociously instilled in a young body, and its converse, a childlike innocence in an aged body – can be blamed for the saccharine tendencies of some religious (and not exclusively Christian) art.[3]

---

1. Valentiner 1937, p. 17, tentatively claimed the drawing to be a portrait of Massimiliano, the son of Ludovico Sforza.
2. Lomazzo 1584, II, ch. VIII.
3. Moffitt 1994.

16

16

LEONARDO DA VINCI

The bust of a youth in right profile, c.1485

Pen and ink, 13.7 × 8.2 cm (5⅜ × 3¼″)
Numbered by Melzi *A/.i.*
RL 12432

This is a good example of Leonardo's standard fine-boned youth before the emergence of the fleshier Salaì/Nero type. The style of the drawing, and sketches of machinery on the verso of the sheet, date it to the mid-1480s. The nose is a little more prominent than usual and the hair more luxuriant, but the subject is a brother of the youths in CAT. I, a sheet of five or so years earlier.

The inscription *A/.i.* establishes that this was the first in a sequence of fifty-two consecutively numbered heads, assembled by Melzi from the drawings of Leonardo that he had inherited.

17

LEONARDO DA VINCI

The head of a youth in right profile, c.1510

Red and black chalks on pale red prepared paper
21.7 × 15.3 cm (8⁹⁄₁₆ × 6″)
Numbered by Melzi *34.*
RL 12554
Exhibited in London only

This is the most elaborately worked of all Leonardo's drawings of youthful heads, in a highly colouristic technique used by the artist for only a few years around 1510. The use of red chalk on red prepared paper limits the tonal contrasts in the face, whereas the black chalk of the hair overlays and mingles with the red in a dense pattern of corkscrews. The long, gently curving horizontal strokes of chalk build up a smoothly rounded surface suggestive of a layer of juvenile fat that has not been shed with the passing of adolescence; the barely defined jaw, merging with the slight pouch of a double chin, the suppressed smile, the straight nose and the untroubled eyes all testify to a life of idle luxury.

34

18

LEONARDO DA VINCI

The bust of a youth in left profile, c.1517–18

Black chalk, 19.3 × 14.9 cm (7⅝ × 5⅞″)
Numbered by Melzi .26.
RL 12557

Like many of Leonardo's bust-length studies, the shoulders here (clad in a low-cut gathered chemise) are turned in three-quarters view while the head remains in strict profile. The profile type is that of Nero as transmitted to the Renaissance through coins and medals; both sides of a bronze *sestertius* of Nero, for instance, were copied by Leonardo on a drawing of *c*.1503–4 (FIG. 14), and the head seen there approximates closely to the conception of the present drawing.[1] The delicacy of the black chalk suggests that this is one of Leonardo's latest drawings, executed during his final residence at the French court in the Loire valley. The contrast between the softly modelled surface and the emphatic outline destroys the illusion of three-dimensional form, draining the image to such a degree that it reads as flat pattern or low relief rather than a body in space.

Attempts have consequently been made to relate drawings such as this to Leonardo's supposed activity as an engraver of gems and cameos in the antique manner. The principal evidence for this activity is a reference in Camillo Lunardi's *Speculum lapidum* (Venice, 1502) to a gem engraver called 'Leonardus mediolanensis' (Leonardo of Milan), a name by which Leonardo da Vinci seems never to have been known.[2] Another possible mention of a carving in relief by Leonardo is in the poem *Antiquarie prospettiche romane composte per prospectivo melanese dipinctore*, a short compendium of the marvels of Rome, dedicated to Leonardo and probably written *c*.1496–8 by an anonymous author who has been variously identified as Bramante, Bramantino or Bernardo Zenale. This includes two references to a work apparently by Leonardo, of a head with a fine neck and head of hair, though it is hard to understand exactly what the poet is describing and the object may not actually have existed.[3] It is hazardous in the extreme to conclude anything from these scanty indications.

1. Cunnally 1988.
2. Manzoni 1881, p. 61; Pedretti 1953, pp. 193–6; Ost 1975; Marani 2000, p. 279. See also Pedretti 1984 on the existence of another artist called Leonardo in Milan in the late fifteenth century.
3. See Pedretti 1989, p. 12, n. 7; Marani 2000, p. 294, n. 16, p. 301, n. 107.

FIG. 14

LEONARDO DA VINCI

Copies of a sestertius of Nero, c.1503–4

Pen and ink over black chalk, area shown 5.5 × 11.2 cm (2³⁄₁₆ × 4⁷⁄₁₆″)
RL 12328v (detail)

19

men) in being bearded; this may be a reflection of the fashion at the court of Francis I, who himself sported a beard.

Whereas the hair in CATS. 17 and 18 hung from the head in ringlets, here it has the character of the waves in Leonardo's late drawings of water, as in his most stylised *Deluges*. The dense curved locks are found throughout antique Roman art and especially in the representations of Hadrian's favourite, Antinous; the overall classicising set of the head has also been compared to the so-called Lucius Verus class of antique busts, examples of which Leonardo could have seen on many occasions.[1]

1.   Clark and Pedretti 1968–9, pp. 102f; Clark 1969, p. 23.

20

Leonardo da Vinci
The bust of a man in right profile, c.1510

Red and black chalks on red prepared paper
22.2 × 15.9 cm (8¾ × 6¼")
RL 12556

In technique, though not in scale, this is a counterpart of CAT. 17. The long smooth strokes of chalk in that drawing are here supplanted by small areas of red chalk lightly rubbed into the surface, strengthened in places by stumping (working the chalk into the paper with a blunt dry tool such as a roll of paper or the finger), by wetting the tip of the chalk, and by accents in black chalk around the features of the face as well as in the hair. These wide variations of surface texture convey wonderfully the sense of slack skin hanging over firm muscle.

19

Leonardo da Vinci
The head of a bearded man in right profile, c.1517–18

Black chalk, 17.8 × 13.0 cm (7 × 5⅛")
Numbered by Melzi .40.
RL 12553

As with CAT. 18, the refined black chalk style is that of Leonardo's latest drawings, when he purged his sheets of the colouristic effects seen in CATS. 17 and 20. The watermark, a fragment of a hand with a flower, is of a type usually (though not exclusively) found in France, and the drawing was probably produced during the last couple of years of Leonardo's life. The head is unusual among his drawings (other than those of old

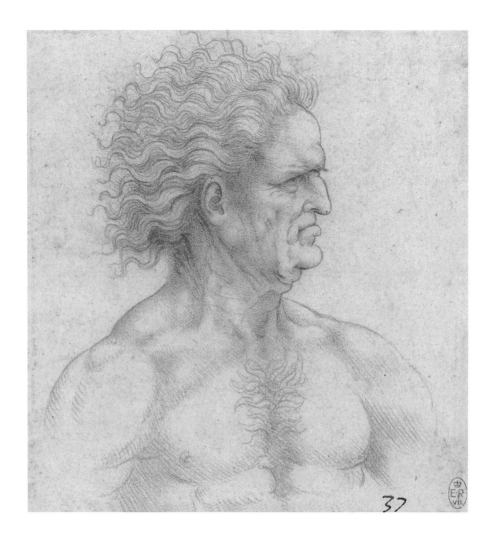

FIG. 15
QUINTEN MASSYS (1465/6–1530)
A bust of Terminus (reverse of medal to Erasmus), c.1525
Bronze, diameter 10.5 cm (4¼")
London, British Museum, Department of Coins and Medals,
inv. 1906-11-3-1529

21

Attributed to FRANCESCO MELZI
(1491/3–c.1570), after Leonardo
*The bust of a man with flowing hair,
the head in right profile*, after c.1510

Red chalk, 12.9 × 12.1 cm (5¹⁄₁₆ × 4¾″)
Numbered by Melzi *37*
RL 12494

The drawing is a faithful copy of a lost original by Leonardo, and is most probably by his pupil and heir Francesco Melzi. There is a marked contrast between the profile head and the almost frontal bust, and the flying hair is distinct from the classically curled style usually found on Leonardo's heads. Both these features are remarkably similar to those of a bust of Terminus on the reverse of a medal of 1519 of the humanist scholar Desiderius Erasmus, and the original of this drawing (or some other copy) may well have served as the model for that bust.

Erasmus had adopted Terminus as his personal device after he was presented by his pupil Alexander Stewart (son of James IV of Scotland) with an antique gem while travelling in Italy in 1509. The gem was carved with a bust in full face that was thought to represent Terminus, the god who defied Jupiter when he cleared the Capitol for his own sanctuary. Erasmus subsequently had a signet seal engraved with a copy of the gem and the legend CONCEDO NULLI ('I yield to none'), and in 1519 the Antwerp artist Quinten Massys designed for Erasmus a medal with a profile of the humanist on the obverse and a bust of Terminus on the reverse (FIG. 15).[1]

The medal shows Terminus as here, a bust turned to the front with the head in profile and a shock of flying hair. There is, however, the complication that in attempting to commission a second version of the medal in 1524 through Willibald Pirckheimer in Nuremberg – all strikings of the first version having been given away – Erasmus suggested turning the head of Terminus to profile 'si caput Termini vertatur ad latus' so that it could be rendered in lower relief.

This would imply that there was a first version of the medal with the bust in full face, as in the gem, though no such medal survives. But it would seem that the attempt to commission a new reverse through Pirckheimer came to nothing, and that Massys himself revised his original design on the basis of Leonardo's invention, for we know that Massys had access to some of Leonardo's creations, probably through the medium of copies (see CATS. 39, 40).

The face of Terminus on the medal is not the warrior type of Leonardo's lost drawing but a finely featured young man. Edgar Wind suggested that this youthfulness referred to two classical accounts (Livy and Dionysius of Halicarnassus) of Terminus' clash with Jove, in which Terminus was joined by the god of youth Juventus; and that by conflating Terminus and Juventus, the figure on the medal signified eternal youth.[2] Flying hair could be a symbol of youth in itself, though this was plainly not intended by Leonardo in the original of the present drawing.

On the verso of the sheet is a ghostly impression of CAT. 22. The two drawings were numbered consecutively by Melzi, and the offset suggests that his method of preserving the drawings was to inlay them and bind them in an album, such that over time chalk from CAT. 22 rubbed off to leave a blurred image on the reverse of the preceding sheet.

1. For Erasmus and Terminus see Wind 1937–8; Panofsky 1969; Rotterdam 1969, pp. 269–71; McConica 1971; Silver 1978; Rowlands 1980.
2. Wind 1937–8, p. 68.

22

LEONARDO DA VINCI
The bust of a man, full face, and the
*head of a lion, c.*1505–10

Red chalk and touches of white chalk on pale
red prepared paper, 18.3 × 13.6 cm (7³⁄₁₆ × 5³⁄₈″)
Numbered by Melzi *38*.
RL 12502

The lion's head appears to have been something of an afterthought, sketched as an addition to an already complete and carefully worked frontal study of Leonardo's favourite type of old man with beetling brow and strongly downturned mouth. It may be part of a skin worn by the man, the pelt swagged from his left shoulder across his chest and his arm through the mouth of the lion. The use of a lion's head as a shoulderpiece was a common motif in classicising costumes of the Renaissance, especially armour,[1] or in any context where lion pelts were worn, such as depictions of Hercules or wild men.[2] Here the extravagant mass of hair and the wreath of ivy leaves (of which the lion's mane is a deliberate echo) would support the idea that a wild man was Leonardo's ostensible subject – he had designed costumes of wild men for a festival in 1491 (see p. 158), though this drawing dates from over a decade after that event and cannot be related. The ivy wreath (like that of oak in CAT. 41) would thus seem to have no particular symbolic meaning.

Leonardo must also have intended, in sketching the lion's head, to draw a parallel between its facial features and those of the man. This theme is already present in CAT. 1 of the late 1470s, and is the principal concern of CAT. 47, where the expressions of fury in horse, man and lion are compared; here the faces are expressionless, and Leonardo's interest lay in the permanent cast of the features. CAT. 22 is therefore one of the very few sheets in Leonardo's oeuvre to manifest an interest in the ancient theory of physiognomics. This was based on the idea that the soul was the essential controlling force of the body, giving it shape, defining character, controlling the fleeting senses of judgement and emotion and giving them their outlet in our gestures and facial expressions. These manifestations of the soul were not infinitely variable but dependent on the balance of the humours – blood,

black bile, yellow bile and phlegm. Each individual had a preponderance of one of these, which led to a certain character type, respectively sanguine (hopeful and confident), melancholic (gloomy), choleric (irascible), or phlegmatic (lethargic).

Certain animals could also be characterised according to this theory, which led to the classification of human faces according to their resemblance to these animals. The lion, for instance, was choleric by nature, and thus choleric men tended facially to resemble lions. The theory was not conceived in the context of art but as a science in its own right, and was not discussed in a treatise on art until 1504, in Pomponius Gauricus' *De sculptura*. Artists rarely exploited any animal-facial type other than the leonine, not least because the lion was one of the few animals whose qualities were generally positive (unlike the wolf, fox, sheep, ox, pig, ass and so on), and there is no comparison in Leonardo's drawings or writings of a man's features with those of any animal other than a lion.

By 1503 Leonardo owned at least three books that dealt directly with physiognomics: an edition of the *Liber Physionomiae* of Michael Scot, first published in 1477; the *Liber Secretorum* of Albertus Magnus, published in Bologna in 1478; and Pliny's *Natural History*.[3] But while Leonardo did not question the medical basis of the humours, he was the only author of the Renaissance to reject explicitly the predictive basis of physiognomical theory (along with chiromancy – see CAT. 41), and there is no evidence that Leonardo had any interest in a programmatic approach to physiognomics.[4]

1. See New York 1998–9, p. 92.
2. Pedretti 1973, p. 80, claiming the subject to be Hercules.
3. See Reti 1968.
4. On Leonardo and physiognomics in general see Meller 1963; Vallese 1992; Kwakkelstein 1994; Laurenza 1996.

23

LEONARDO DA VINCI
The bust of a man, full face, c.1505–10

Red chalk (rubbed) with touches of black chalk
on red prepared paper, 17.8 × 13.6 cm (7 × 5⅜″)
Numbered by Melzi .22.
RL 12503

The face is a virtual repetition of CAT. 22, though the
man is balding and the creases in his face are less pronounced (this is not just a consequence of the rubbing
of the sheet). He thus appears pathetic rather than
fierce, and this may have been Leonardo's intention in
making the drawing – to examine how small changes
in the features can lead to substantial changes in the
character conveyed.

A very similar head was engraved at an early date
by Giovanni Antonio da Brescia (FIG. 16).[1] Such engravings, drawn copies and, most probably, sculpted busts
were instrumental in making the features of Leonardo's
favourite old man familiar to a generation of followers
(FIG. 17),[2] whose frequently unthinking adoption of the
type, especially in religious paintings, was among the
more monotonous features of early sixteenth-century
Lombard art.

1.   Hind 1948, V, p. 86, no. 4.
2.   See Kwakkelstein 1993a and 1994, pp. 123–31.

FIG. 16 *(above)*
GIOVANNI ANDREA DA BRESCIA (fl. *c.*1490–1525),
after Leonardo
The head of an old man, c.1510–20
Engraving, 13.4 × 10.0 cm (5¼ × 3¹⁵⁄₁₆″)
Vienna, Albertina

FIG. 17
FOLLOWER OF LEONARDO
The head of an old man with long hair, c.1520(?)
Wash, pen and ink, white bodycolour, over black chalk,
on paper washed brown, 21.6 × 17.7 cm (8½ × 6¹⁵⁄₁₆″)
RL 12501

24

LEONARDO DA VINCI

The head of an old bearded man, in right profile, c.1510–18

Black chalk, 21.3 × 15.5 cm (8⅜ × 6⅛")
Numbered by Melzi *.29*
RL 12499

Though the profile is Leonardo's usual toothless old man, he is here far from pitiful. The neck is vigorously muscular, the beard luxuriant, and the long hair is twisted into plaits reminiscent of the *Leda* of the previous decade (CATS. 58–61) or of Verrocchio's drawings of many years before (FIG. 47, p. 144). The hair suggests that Leonardo intended a certain exoticism, as if the man were an oriental magus,[1] and the conspicuously hooked nose would be in keeping with such a conception.

The drawing can be dated to the last decade of Leonardo's life. We know that Leonardo himself had a full beard at this time (see CAT. 46), and an old bearded man drawing an old bearded man cannot have been oblivious to an element of self-portraiture. Indeed a copy of the drawing executed by Lucas Vorsterman in the 1620s, soon after it arrived in England, is inscribed as a portrait of Leonardo, reflecting the common conception (by then fully established) of Leonardo as a mystical seer.[2]

1. Silver 1984, p. 91, no. 40, suggested that Quinten Massys adopted the type of CATS. 24–5 for his 1526 *Adoration of the Magi*, though the resemblance seems no more than generic.
2. British Museum, inv. 5227–4; Roberts (forthcoming), fig. 6.

25

LEONARDO DA VINCI

The head of an old bearded man,
in left profile, c.1517–18

Black chalk on rough paper
25.3 × 18.2 cm (9⁵⁄₁₆ × 7³⁄₁₆″)
Numbered by Melzi .47.
RL 12500

The drawing is on the thick, mealy, low-quality paper often used by Leonardo in the last years of his life in France (cf. CATS. 71–3). Lank hair hangs from the back of the bald cranium, the lips are parted to reveal a couple of peg-like teeth, and the nose was drawn repeatedly to make it progressively more bulbous and pendulous. Again, Leonardo must have been conscious here of some element of self-portraiture, even self-caricature. When Cardinal Luigi of Aragon visited Leonardo in France in October 1517, his secretary Antonio de Beatis reported that Leonardo was more than 70 years old (he was actually 66, though exaggeration of age was common at that time) and that 'a certain paralysis has crippled his right hand'. Leonardo would live for another eighteen months, and it seems that his last years were marked by a slow decline of health. A drawing such as this, with no preparatory purpose and retained by the artist, surely expresses some of Leonardo's feelings about his own physical decay.

THE GROTESQUE

Just as beauty resulted from the harmony of the parts, so ugliness was a consequence of their discord. Leonardo's repeated drawing of the youthful head, and the recurrence of a single facial type that is such a feature of Leonardo's later paintings, were attempts to hone the precise relationships that constituted one perfect beauty; but there were many different uglinesses, and his grotesque heads were in essence an investigation of these.

The grotesque in art could serve several purposes. It could be simply decorative, and there was a rich tradition of monstrous fantasy in the margins of medieval manuscripts and the carvings of Romanesque and Gothic churches. It could act as a foil to something beautiful, exploiting the device of antithesis discussed under CAT. 27; Leonardo recommended that the painter place 'the ugly next to the beautiful, the big to the small, the old to the young, the strong to the weak, all should be varied as much as possible and close together.'[1] But the most meaningful use of ugliness was as a sign of degeneracy, and this could be either comic or evil.

The grotesque face as a mark of evil is found throughout European art. Devils and demons gave the artist a welcome freedom to concoct monstrous heads. Scenes of the Passion of Christ – the Mocking, Christ carrying the Cross, the Crucifixion and so on – and of the martyrdom of saints routinely contrast the divinely beautiful holy figure with an array of ugly tormentors. Grotesque figures (usually old women) could personify vice, as seen in Albrecht Dürer's *Avarice* (Vienna, Kunsthistorisches Museum), Andrea Mantegna's *Pallas expelling the Vices from the Garden of Virtue* (Paris, Musée du Louvre), and in one of Leonardo's allegorical drawings at Christ Church, Oxford, where a decrepit old satyress as a symbol of evil is repulsed by Justice and Prudence in the form of beautiful maidens.[2]

The comic-grotesque was less uniformly spread through Italian art than the evil-grotesque, and was far less extensive in scope than the parallel tradition of humorous tales and songs. Works such as Giovanni Boccaccio's *Decameron* and Poggio Bracciolini's *Facetie* (a copy of which Leonardo owned and emulated), the repertoire of *canti carnascialeschi* (carnival songs), and the satirical poems that mocked the repetitive conventions of courtly love poetry could all have provided rich material for the visual arts.[3] But Italian comic art of the fifteenth century shows little sign of the complex and often sympathetic treatment of the human condition found in contemporary literary sources, and its fascination with the merely bizarre or deformed owes more to northern visual prototypes. Early Italian prints occasionally have a grotesque element influenced by the earthy and widely circulated Flemish and German prints of the period, and the cheap Flemish wall-hangings listed in Florentine inventories would routinely have included amusing details and scenes of daily (low-)life.[4]

From the (admittedly patchy) surviving evidence it does not appear that Leonardo had any special interest in humorous art or the grotesque during his early years in Florence. He has been associated with a curious series of drawings of dancing figures in the Uffizi and a related engraving apparently of a morris dance, though this association is very much an extrapolation from his later interests.[5] It was not until Leonardo had moved to Milan that the comic-grotesque appeared in his art as a coherent theme, and far more of the overtly grotesque and comic heads date from the mid-1480s through the early 1490s than from any other phase of his career.

Leonardo's earliest grotesques are small pen sketches (CATS. 31–6), exploring the permanent expressionless structure of the face, which he conceived for didactic purposes as composed of four zones, the forehead, nose, mouth and chin.[6] Most of Leonardo's grotesque heads are no more than playful distortions of these four elements, which explains the 'strange uniformity, even monotony, behind the surface of extreme variations' that Ernst Gombrich perceived.[7] The more elaborate grotesques mostly date from the early 1490s, the period during which Leonardo was assembling material towards his treatise on painting, and more specifically when he was most concerned with attempting to establish the proportions of the face (CAT. 4); the idea that the face could be perfectly proportioned had its corollary in the games that the artist could play by deliberately distorting these proportions.

This goes some way to explaining the form of Leonardo's grotesque heads, but it does not explain their purpose. They were clearly meant to be entertaining, and the degree of elaboration of some of the drawings (CATS. 39–41) would suggest that they were created not only for Leonardo's amusement but for an audience. How the tastes of the Sforza court might have influenced this strand of Leonardo's art is not known, but those grotesques that do have an ostensible subject are sophisticated rather than crude; several are satirical, mocking the vanity of the aged, which Leonardo clearly found more deserving of ridicule than simple deformity. But Leonardo was careful to keep the grotesque out of his paintings, for while a grotesque drawing could be an entertaining sample of an artist's ingenuity, it had no place in an enterprise as intrinsically serious as painting. The *St Jerome* in the Vatican and some of the heads in the *Last Supper* approach Leonardo's favourite type of wizened old man, but none is distorted in the manner of the drawings in the following section. There is nothing in Leonardo's oeuvre as coarse as the celebrated painting by the early fifteenth-century Milanese artist Michelino da Besozzo, now lost but described in detail by Gian Paolo Lomazzo and lovingly emulated by later sixteenth-century Lombard painters, of four peasants groping each other and laughing uproariously.[8] Laughter was acceptable in children, but in adults – especially when showing the teeth – it was the sign of peasants, harlots, drunkards, the dishonest, and fools in general; and the trap of comic art was that by laughing at a ridiculous scene one was reduced to the same state of ridiculousness.[9]

In some ways, what Leonardo's grotesque heads are *not* is more notable than what they are. As explained elsewhere (p. 13 and CAT. 22), they are not studies towards a systematic treatment of human physiognomy, nor are they studies for his paintings. With few exceptions they are not caricatures, in the true sense of an exaggeration of an individual's features to produce an intensified likeness (the word derives from the Italian *ritratto caricato*, charged or loaded portrait).[10] There was no coherent tradition of caricature before the Carracci family of artists and their followers in Bologna and Rome around 1600, and very few of Leonardo's head studies can reasonably be taken to be the comically

FIG. 18
LEONARDO DA VINCI
A caricature of an Italian official(?), 1517
Pen and ink, 4.1 × 2.7 cm (1⅝ × 1¹⁄₁₆″)
RL 12470

distorted depictions of individuals. A small but obvious example is found on a fragment at Windsor (FIG. 18), cut from a sheet in the Codex Atlanticus (f. 103r-b) that bears the date May 1517. Leonardo was at that time resident in France, and the typically Italian headgear of the man suggests that he was a visitor to the French court. But such drawings are exceptional in Leonardo's oeuvre, and the underlying consistency of his creatures demonstrates that they are in general imaginary rather than playful manipulations of reality.

Further, Leonardo's grotesque heads are not studies in pathological deformity. He would of course have seen excessively prominent or receding chins, for instance, and the toothlessness and other effects of ageing that he took delight in drawing, but Leonardo had no interest in hunchbacks, dwarves, goitres, warts, nor any of the other deformities that commonly passed as amusing; indeed he dismissed them as a worthwhile subject for the *Treatise*, stating 'of monstrous faces I do not speak, as they are remembered without difficulty'. He twice drew monstrous births, a thoracoparasite and a hare or rabbit with conjoined heads and thoraxes and two distinct abdomens,[11] but these were treated with scientific fascination rather than amused disgust, and the belief that such monstrosities were portents is absent from Leonardo's writings.

It must be concluded that no programme lay behind Leonardo's interest in the comic-grotesque, and as a genre it probably occupied his attention much less than posterity has wished to believe. Beyond a burst of activity around 1490, drawings of the grotesque are scattered through Leonardo's oeuvre with little common purpose other than a delight in the potential of his pen to create form, and each sheet must be taken on its own terms rather than being forced into some overarching scheme.

CAT. 41 (detail)

1. Codex Urbinas, f. 61v; McMahon 1956, no. 271.
2. Popham 1946, no. 105.
3. For the satirical poets see Bontempelli 1922; for the *canti carnascialeschi*, Singleton 1936; for Leonardo's books, Kemp 1984–5.
4. For the northern sources of Italian comic art see Meijer 1998.
5. On the dancers and the print see Tietze-Conrat 1957, pp. 94f.; Florence 1992, nos 5.1–4; Dillon 1994; Kwakkelstein 1994, p. 19; Kwakkelstein 1998; Lugano 1998, nos 1–2.
6. Codex Urbinas f. 108v; McMahon 1956, no. 416.
7. Gombrich 1976, p. 64.
8. Lomazzo 1584, VI, ch. XXXII. See Meijer 1971, p. 259; Paliaga 1995b.
9. Miedema 1977; Aronberg Lavin 1981.
10. Gombrich and Kris 1952.
11. Respectively Codex Atlanticus f. 14r-b (see Belloni 1954) and Milan, Biblioteca Ambrosiana, inv. F. 263 inf. 7; Milan 1998–9b, no. 16. Belloni 1982, discussing Leonardo's interest in deformity, rather demonstrated that such interest was minimal.

26

LEONARDO DA VINCI

A bearded man in left profile, confronted by a grotesque profile, c.1492–5

Pen and ink, 17.2 × 12.4 cm (6¾ × 4⅞″)
Numbered by Melzi .8.

RL 12555V

The disdainful expression of the main figure is deflated by the rapidly sketched grotesque profile that gazes up at him from heavy-lidded bulging eyes. While it is doubtful if Leonardo rationalised his impulse to sketch such inconsequential profiles, an opposition of types may here have been intended to some degree – aquiline against snub nose, hideously long upper lip against tightly compact mouth – but this is not fully cogitated and cannot have been the main reason for drawing either figure. The addition of the grotesque was the work of no more than a few seconds, a simple visual joke that may have been an impromptu satire on double portraits of couples in facing profile; the effect is disconcertingly similar to that in Filippo Lippi's *Portrait of a woman with a man at a window* (New York, Metropolitan Museum of Art),[1] but it is doubtful that Leonardo would have known that portrait during his years in Florence, or even that he would have had a specific model in mind when sketching in the grotesque here.

A note on the other side of the sheet reads 'When you make a figure, think well about what it is and what you want it to do, and see that the work is in keeping with the figure's aim and character.' This has been taken as support for the often stated idea that the main figure is a study of a semitic type for the Apostles (and especially Judas) in the *Last Supper*.[2] It does not, however, have the character of a preparatory study for a painting, and is likely to be no more than a typical exercise in Leonardo's mature type, severe in aspect, bald and with an odd forward-swept beard. On the other side of the sheet the head was traced through in red chalk, and while doubts have been cast on the authorship of the red-chalk tracing it seems to be an example of Leonardo's tentative early efforts with the medium.[3]

1. Washington 2001–2, no. 3.
2. See Pedretti 1983–6, no. 4.
3. A drawing made by Lucas Vorsterman when CAT. 26 was in the Arundel collection (British Museum, inv. 5227–67) copies both sides of the sheet in the same traced-through relationship to each other; see Roberts (forthcoming), figs. 7–11.

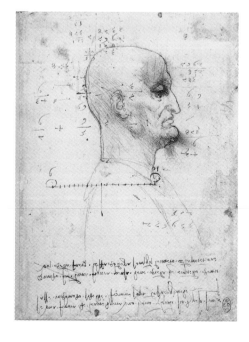

CAT. 26 (recto)

27

LEONARDO DA VINCI
Two grotesque profiles confronted, c.1485–90

Pen and ink with wash, 16.3 × 14.3 cm (6⁷⁄₁₆ × 5⅝″)
Numbered by Melzi .52.
RL 12490

This is one of the finest examples of Leonardo's fierce old men, the vigorous strokes of the pen blocking out his spare and deeply lined features with a strongly exaggerated brow and chin. Unusually among the grotesques, the profile was finished with areas of wash. Facing him is the hideously fleshy profile of an old woman, her hair drawn back and her left arm tucked under a bosom trussed tightly so that her breasts bulge out above the bodice. She is the embodiment of aged vanity, seen again in CATS. 36, 39 and 40.

A contrast between bony and fleshy types was surely intended by Leonardo. The juxtaposition of two contrary motifs (of any kind) in order to explore and magnify each one was a standard rhetorical device, known in Greek as *antithesis* and in Latin as *contrapositum*. The Italian term, *contrapposto*, is now applied exclusively to the visual arts, to describe the method of posing a body so that the parts are in balanced opposition to one another; but in the Renaissance it could still be applied to the more general requirement to formulate a composition with many different elements in lively counterpoint – the insistence on variety found in all treatises on the arts.[1] Michael Kwakkelstein and Domenico Laurenza went further and interpreted the two figures as embodiments of humoral types, the former seeing them as choleric and melancholic, the latter as choleric and phlegmatic. The fact that, even with such an emphatic example of opposed profiles, two scholars should differ on the reading of the figures cautions against the validity of such interpretations.[2]

The difference in scale between the two figures indicates that Leonardo did not initially conceive of them as interacting, and that the gesture of the old woman, holding her hand to the chin of the man in a romantic manner, was an afterthought. But by uniting the two figures in this manner Leonardo turned them into a pair of ridiculous aged lovers, the subject treated again in CAT. 40, and thus a parody of the opposed profiles of married couples that (in diptych form) was one of the standard modes of fifteenth-century portraiture.

1. See Summers 1981, pp. 76–80 etc; Moffitt 1994. Moffitt's suggestions that the 'original significance' of Leonardo's head studies was 'primarily as theoretical expressions conceived according to the wholly conventionalised modes of classical rhetoric', and that the term *contrapposti* rather than *grotteschi* therefore be used for them, are not warranted.
2. Kwakkelstein 1994, p. 114; Laurenza 1996, p. 18, seeing the same types in CAT. 31.

28

29

28

LEONARDO DA VINCI

A bald fat man with a broken nose, in right profile, c.1485–90

Pen and ink
16.0 × 13.5 cm (6⁵⁄₁₆ × 5⁵⁄₁₆″), upper left corner cut
Numbered by Melzi .24.
RL 12489

The roughness and vigour with which the pen is handled dates the drawing to the late 1480s. The corpulent figure is not one of Leonardo's usual types, and the obvious speed with which it was drawn suggests that this may be a sketch of a specific individual with the nose and lower lip exaggerated for comic effect, and thus one of Leonardo's very few true caricatures.

29

LEONARDO DA VINCI

A grotesque old man in right profile, c.1490–95

Red and black chalks, pen and ink
15.9 × 9.3 cm (6¼ × 3¹¹⁄₁₆″)
Numbered by Melzi .13.
RL 12448

In depictions of the Mocking of Christ and similar scenes, an oversized hat could be a sign of 'otherness' and thus implicitly sinister or evil; here it is merely amusing.[1] The combination of red and black chalks with pen and ink is unusually elaborate for a drawing of this type, and it has been suggested that the red chalk is later, by a pupil.[2] The hatching of the red chalk is left-handed, however, and seems to be in the scratchy manner of Leonardo's early attempts to exploit the medium. The hard-to-read scribble of an eye in the right margin is certainly not by Leonardo.

1. See Mellinkoff 1993, pp. 89–91, on outsized hats.
2. Clark and Pedretti 1968–9, p. 73.

30

LEONARDO DA VINCI

*A grotesque old man leaning on a stick,
and a man's back, c.1510–15*

Pen and ink on blue paper
7.7 × 12.3 cm (3¹⁄₁₆ × 4¹³⁄₁₆″), top corners cut
Numbered by Melzi *.21.*
RL 12488 (Keele and Pedretti 1979, no. 189)

There were small but significant Jewish communities in many Italian cities of the period, and the late fifteenth century had seen a wave of antisemitic sentiment inflamed by itinerant preachers such as Fra Bernardino da Feltre, ostensibly on the grounds of usury but spiced with accusations of the ritual murder of Christian children. While actual violence against Jews had died down by the early sixteenth century – often suppressed by the ruling classes, who recognised the economic importance of the Jewish banks – their popular reputation as grasping moneylenders undoubtedly persisted. A degree of hostility (rather than simple caricature) is often visible in the depiction of Jews in scenes from the Passion of Christ, and Leonardo here shows himself no less susceptible to the stereotype than any other artist. The old man conforms to the caricatured Jewish type more strongly than in any other drawing by Leonardo, with a long hooked nose, fleshy lips, avaricious eyes and a claw-like hand clutching a stick.

This type of rough blue paper was frequently used by Leonardo for his very late anatomical drawings, and alongside the grotesque is a sketch of a back with the superficial muscles exaggerated.

FRAGMENTS (CATS. 31–6)

Among Leonardo's drawings at Windsor are several dozen tiny drawings on pieces of paper sometimes no bigger than a postage stamp, many of which can be matched with irregular holes in the pages of the Codex Atlanticus in the Biblioteca Ambrosiana, Milan, the other great assemblage of Leonardo's papers besides that at Windsor. They were most probably cut from those sheets by Leonardo's pupil and heir Francesco Melzi in his attempts to organise Leonardo's papers, and most bear a small number, apparently in Melzi's hand, in a sequence running from 1 to 69.

Melzi was assiduous in gleaning profiles and other head studies from the sheets that went to form the Codex Atlanticus – there are very few remaining small profiles to be found on those sheets, and most of those are not by Leonardo. He did not, however, excise the many small profiles to be found on the sheets now at Windsor. This suggests that the separation of the drawings into technological (Codex Atlanticus) and non-technological (Windsor) studies was due to Melzi and not to Pompeo Leoni, the subsequent owner of the drawings, who must therefore have largely preserved Melzi's arrangement when binding his Leonardo drawings into albums.

The parent sheets of the fragments, where they can be identified, are mostly large folios of miscellaneous studies drawn in the studio, not pages from the notebooks that Leonardo advocated the artist should carry around in order to record impressions of individuals in the street.[1] Further, all the sketched heads are in pen and ink, which would have been impractical to use 'on the hoof'; metalpoint (especially leadpoint, which leaves a trace on unprepared paper) was much more convenient for that sort of impromptu sketch. This only confirms what might be supposed from the forms of the heads themselves, that they were in general drawn from Leonardo's imagination rather than from the life.

1.   Codex Urbinas, f. 60v.

31

LEONARDO DA VINCI
*Two grotesque profiles confronted, c.*1485–90

Pen and ink, 4.2 × 5.0 cm ($1\frac{5}{8}$ × $1\frac{15}{16}''$)
Numbered by Melzi 37.
RL 12474

Despite its modest size, this sketch is one of the clearest examples of contrasting profiles in the whole of Leonardo's oeuvre. A head with grotesquely beetling brow, screwed-up eyes, flattened nose and protruding chin faces a profile with sloping forehead, bulging eyelids, a long hooked nose and a receding chin. The parent sheet has not been identified with certainty.

32

LEONARDO DA VINCI
*A man in right profile, c.*1503–4

Pen and ink, 5.2 × 5.0 cm ($2\frac{1}{16}$ × $1\frac{15}{16}''$)
Numbered by Melzi 7.
RL 12459

The drawing was cut from a sheet in the Codex Atlanticus (f. 252v-a) that mainly studies methods of surveying mountains. The bust was drawn over a scribble of two peaks, and a straight line between their summits passes through the nape of the man's neck. The numbers to the right are fragments of calculations on the parent sheet.

33

LEONARDO DA VINCI
The bust of an old man, c.1485

Pen and ink, 6.8 × 4.8 cm (2¹¹⁄₁₆ × 1⅞″)
RL 12457

This is an early example of the decrepit old man, with toothless mouth and sagging flesh, who is found sporadically throughout Leonardo's drawings. The fragment was cut from Codex Atlanticus f. 31r-a, a sheet of studies of military machines datable to early in Leonardo's first Milanese period.

34

LEONARDO DA VINCI
A grotesque man in right profile, with a sugar-loaf hat, c.1485

Pen and ink, 6.6 × 3.4 cm (2⅝ × 1⁵⁄₁₆″)
Numbered by Melzi *33*
RL 12462

Like CATS. 33 and 36, the fragment was cut from a sheet in the Codex Atlanticus (in this case f. 52r-c) containing studies mainly of military machines, dating from the mid-1480s. A number of variant copies of the head are known: in a black chalk drawing in the Pierpont Morgan Library, New York, where the figure is drawn half-length and carries a stick over his left shoulder;[1] in the Ambrosiana;[2] in the Spencer Album, New York Public Library;[3] and, with the profile altered, as one half of a grotesque couple in an engraving by Hans Liefrinck.[4] These copies must have been made after Melzi had excised the profile from the parent sheet, for otherwise it would hardly have been noticed among the mass of Leonardo's technical drawings.

1. Pedretti 1988b; Trutty-Coohill 1993a, no. 13, both regarding the Pierpont Morgan drawing as by Leonardo.
2. Milan, Biblioteca Ambrosiana, inv. F. 274 inf. 26.
3. Trutty-Coohill 1993a, no. 55, II.45.
4. Muylle 1994, fig. 2.

35

LEONARDO DA VINCI
Two grotesque profiles confronted, c.1485

Pen and ink, 6.3 × 6.6 cm (2½ × 2⅝″)
Numbered by Melzi *32*.
RL 12463

As in CAT. 31, Leonardo has juxtaposed extremes of the facial features: snub versus aquiline nose, sucked-in versus protruding fleshy lips, jutting versus receding chin. The parent sheet of the fragment has not been identified.

36

LEONARDO DA VINCI
Two grotesque profiles confronted, c.1485

Pen and ink, 6.5 × 7.0 cm (2⁹⁄₁₆ × 2¾″)
Numbered by Melzi *36*.
RL 12453

The old woman with a high headdress and low-cut dress is the personification of aged vanity, as exemplified in CAT. 39. Her perfectly curved profile is opposed to the flattened profile of a peasant with a thick shock of hair. Like CAT. 33, the drawing was cut from Codex Atlanticus f. 31r-a, and portions of the military machines on the parent sheet intrude upon the fragment at upper centre and lower right.

31

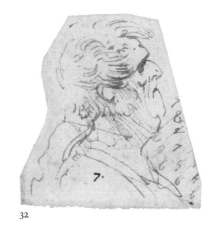

32

33

34

35

36

37

Attributed to FRANCESCO MELZI
(1491/3–*c*.1570), after Leonardo
Five grotesque and three profile heads,
*c.*1510–20(?)

Pen and ink over red chalk, 21.8 × 15.3 cm (8⁹⁄₁₆ × 6″)
Numbered by Melzi *.19.*
RL 12491

Countless copies of Leonardo's grotesque heads survive, usually singly but occasionally lined up as here.
Many of these are copies of an extensive and homo-
geneous sequence of carefully finished heads that
Leonardo seems to have drawn around 1490; several
survive as individual studies, mostly at (or formerly at)
Chatsworth House in Derbyshire. Their original form
is hard to determine, given the habit of later copyists
of grouping them in pairs and larger groups, as here,
but an assemblage of copies arranged as eleven pairs
and one trio, formerly in the Pembroke collection and
now dispersed, may record the original appearance of
a number of Leonardo's creations.[1] Such carefully
drawn copies are hard to attribute with confidence, but
the present sheet, two closely comparable sheets in
the Accademia, Venice (FIG. 19 and FIG. 20, overleaf),
another in the British Museum[2], and the ex-Pembroke
collage are all probably by the hand of Leonardo's
pupil and heir, Francesco Melzi.

The first two heads are a study in morphological
opposites, as in CATS. 31 and 35. A sloping forehead is set
opposite a beetling brow, a long pointed nose against a
flat nose, tightly drawn-in lips against a slack lower lip,
and lank straight hair against tightly curled short hair.
The ape-like creature at upper right, with a monstrous
lip and hair pulled back to a headdress, is an extreme
example of Leonardo's ugly old women, and is one of
the few genuinely disturbing, rather than simply
comic, of Leonardo's grotesque heads. The originals
of these three are not known.

The central three heads are copied after drawings
in the Ambrosiana, the latter two after the same prototype, though his hair in the original is rather sparser
and less schematically curly.[3] There is nothing grotesque about these heads, though the hat worn by the
first is exaggeratedly large and was probably intended

FIG. 19
Attributed to FRANCESCO MELZI (1491/3–*c*.1570),
after Leonardo
*Five heads, c.*1510–20(?)
Pen and ink, 18.0 × 12.0 cm (7¹⁄₁₆ × 4¾″)
Venice, Galleria dell'Accademia, inv. 227

as a joke on bourgeois affectation. The two bottom
figures are also after drawings in the Ambrosiana;[4] the
woman at lower right is another satire on aged vanity.
Her conch-like hairstyle is reminiscent of the elaborate coiffures of the ideal heads produced in Florence
during Leonardo's youth, by Verrocchio and his
contemporaries (FIG. 49, p. 144).

1. Trutty-Coohill 1993a, no. 30.
2. British Museum, inv. 1886-6-9-40.
3. Milan, Biblioteca Ambrosiana, inv. F. 263 inf. 87, F. 271 inf. 17;
    Milan 1982a, nos 6, 8; Milan 1998–9b, nos 19, 21.
4. Biblioteca Ambrosiana, inv. F. 274 inf. 31, 21.

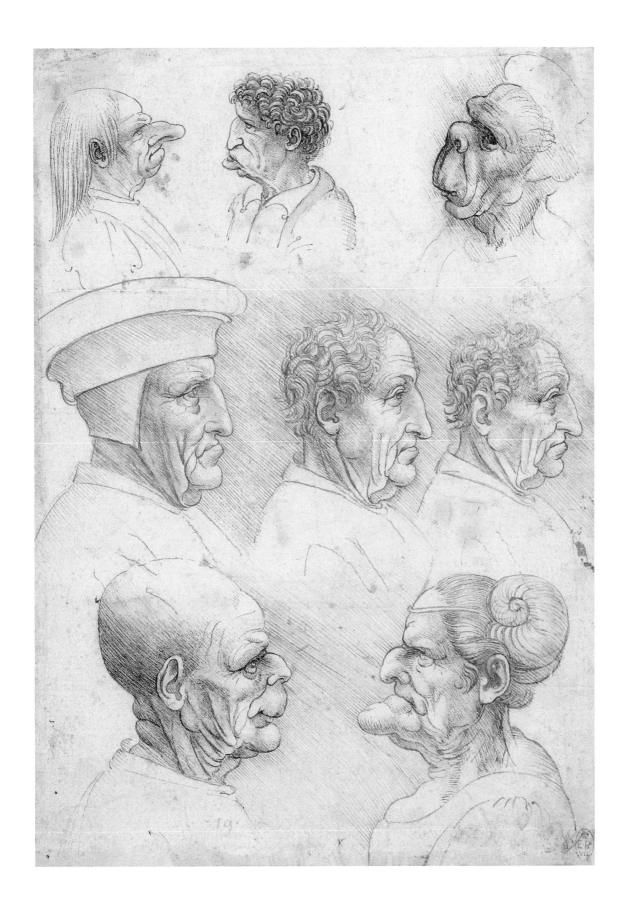

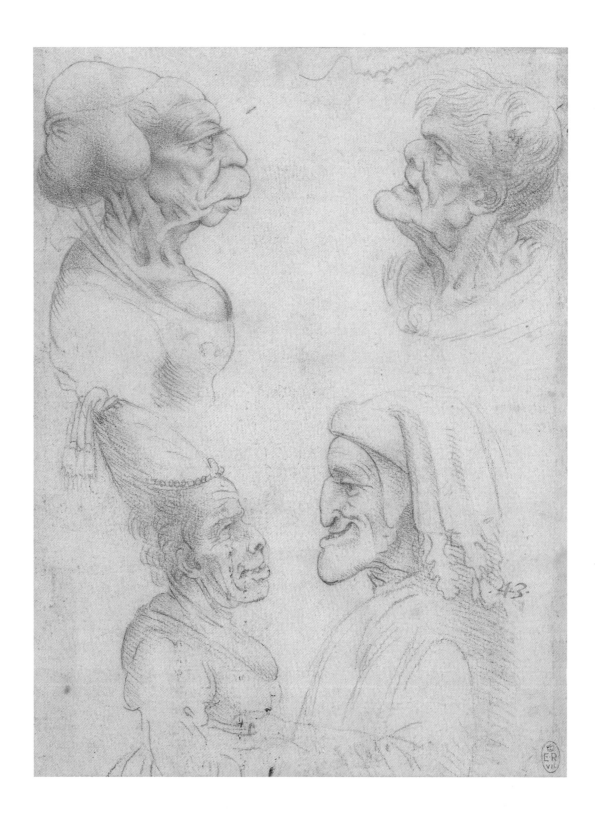

38

Attributed to FRANCESCO MELZI (1491/3–c.1570), after Leonardo
Four grotesque heads, including a caricature of Dante, c.1517–20

Red chalk, 19.5 × 14.6 cm (7¹¹⁄₁₆ × 5¾″)
Numbered by Melzi .43.
RL 12493

Like CAT. 37, this is an assemblage of Leonardo's creatures by a copyist, again probably Francesco Melzi. The sheet bears no watermark but the close chain lines of the paper suggest that it is French, and thus probably used when Melzi was in France with Leonardo at the end of the artist's life, almost thirty years after the originals had been drawn.

The couple below are a rare example of identifiable characters among Leonardo's grotesques. He is a caricature of the standard likeness of Dante, given an idiotic grin as he places his hand on the waist of his sweetheart. The original of Dante is at Chatsworth,[1] a sheet that has been cut down such that his arms cannot now be seen, but their interaction here is too felicitous to be a copyist's intervention. The crone is therefore presumably a parody of Dante's Beatrice.

The original of the old man (or woman?) at upper right, in the Kunsthalle, Hamburg,[2] is pricked around the outlines to transfer the design to another sheet, but there is no trace of pounce marks here. The original of the woman at upper left is not known. These two grotesques were engraved as a couple (with altered hair) by Hans Liefrinck in the mid-sixteenth century,[3] though there is nothing to suggest that Leonardo conceived them as such and Liefrinck was presumably working from a copy such as this in which the two were juxtaposed.

1. Jaffé 1994, no. 890. The two figures are separated in the Spencer Album (Trutty-Coohill 1993b, no. 55, I.11 and I.14), but as they seem to have been copied from the present sheet this separation has no evidential value. Another copy, again at Chatsworth (Jaffé 1994, no. 892c), shows the arms of the two figures similarly intertwined.
2. Popham 1946, no. 134A.
3. Muylle 1994, fig. 1.

FIG. 20
Attributed to FRANCESCO MELZI (1491/3–c.1570), after Leonardo
Seven heads, c.1510–20(?)
Pen and ink, 18.0 × 12.0 cm (7¹⁄₁₆ × 4¾″)
Venice, Galleria dell'Accademia, inv. 229

39

Attributed to FRANCESCO MELZI (1491/3–c.1570), after Leonardo
The bust of a grotesque old woman, c.1510–20(?)

Red chalk, 17.2 × 14.3 cm (6¾ × 5⅝″)
Numbered by Melzi *.32.*
RL 12492

The drawing is again a copy, probably by Melzi, of a lost original by Leonardo of around 1490. The woman is an embodiment of foolish pride and vanity, with a ridiculous contrast between her aged ugliness and her ostentatious and outmoded headdress and tightly laced bodice. Such vanity was scathingly denounced by Erasmus in his *Praise of Folly* (1511):

> It is even more amusing to see these old women, so ancient they might as well be dead .... They pay a good price for the services of some handsome young Adonis. They never cease smearing their faces with make-up. They can't tear themselves away from the mirror .... They show off their withered and flabby breasts .... Everyone laughs at these things as utterly foolish (and indeed they are), but the old bags themselves are perfectly self-satisfied.[1]

The same creature was also drawn in profile by Leonardo, in a quick pen sketch, now sadly cut down (FIG. 21), that presumably preceded this more cogitated three-quarters view.[2] Like several other of Leonardo's grotesque inventions, both these versions of the old woman were known to Quinten Massys in Antwerp. A variant of the profile appears at the left of the several versions of the *Grotesque betrothal* (FIG. 26), and he reproduced the present three-quarters view in a painting in the National Gallery, London (FIG. 22), extending the bust to include her hands resting on a parapet and holding out a rosebud.[3] The London painting can stand as a self-sufficient image, with the rosebud a pathetic symbol of her lost youth. But Massys also painted a pendant of a man in profile, corresponding in size, background colour and the presence of the parapet,[4] and together Massys's two panels form a narrative in

FIG. 21 *(left)*
LEONARDO DA VINCI
A bust of a grotesque old woman in right profile, c.1490
Pen and ink, 10.4 × 8.4 cm (4⅛ × 3⁵⁄₁₆″)
RL 12447

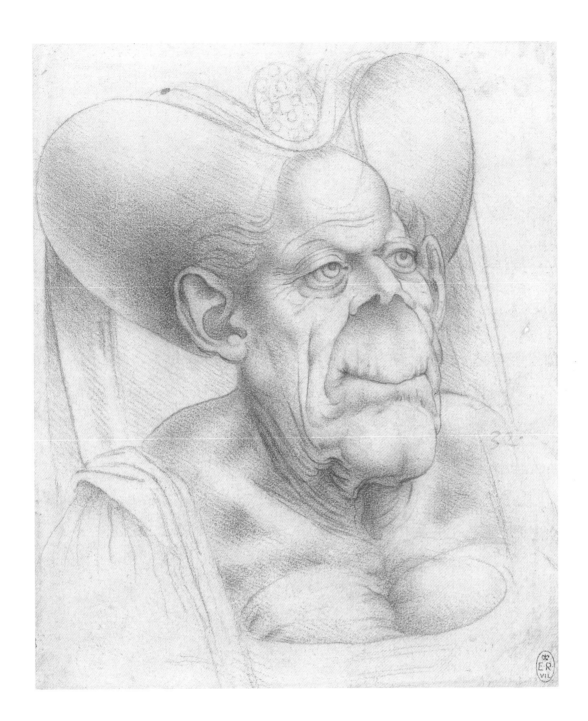

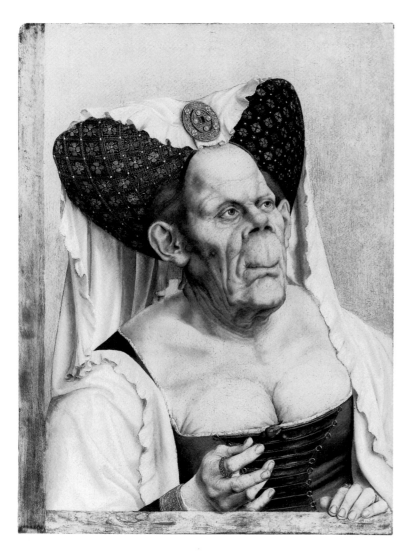

which the man appears to decline the rosebud offered by the woman, a variant of the subject treated by Leonardo himself in CAT. 40.

The couple seen in Massys's panels were etched by Wenceslaus Hollar, probably in the 1640s, with the inscription *Rex et Regina de Tunis. Leonardo da Vinci inv.* ('King and Queen of Tunis. Invented by Leonardo'; FIG. 23).[5] The title seems to be a seventeenth-century fabrication; more interesting is the implication that Leonardo was responsible for the whole invention, the man as well as the woman. Hollar etched several compositions with an ascription to Leonardo of which the originals cannot now be traced, and some of these may in fact have been inventions by Hollar himself in the manner of Leonardo; here, however, he must have had access either to Massys's pair of panels (or variants), with the knowledge that at least one half derived from Leonardo, or to a more directly Leonardesque model that included the old man. There is no profile in Leonardo's surviving work like that of the old man,

FIG. 22

QUINTEN MASSYS (1465/6–1530)
A bust of a grotesque old woman, c.1520
Oil on panel, 64.1 × 45.4 cm (25¼ × 17⅞")
London, National Gallery

FIG. 23

WENCESLAUS HOLLAR (1607–77), after Leonardo
'The King and Queen of Tunis', c.1645
Etching, plate 6.7 × 12.3 cm (2⅝ × 3¹³⁄₁₆")

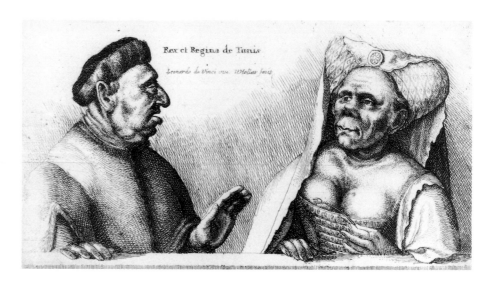

but the depiction of a profile head is exceptional in Netherlandish art of the period and does suggest an Italian model.[6] A variant by Massys of the figure as an embodiment of Avarice,[7] with conspicuously opulent rings and furs, has features that strongly resemble those of Cosimo de' Medici as seen in mid-fifteenth-century portrait medallions, and whether or not Massys knew or intended that identity, this further supports the impression that he was working in emulation of (though not necessarily copying) an Italian source.

It is thus possible that Leonardo did indeed produce a head of an old man as a pendant to his old woman, and that this man was recognisable as a caricature of Cosimo de' Medici. While it would normally be unthinkable for an Italian implicitly to mock his home city in this manner, Leonardo had caricatured Florence's favourite son Dante in the original of CAT. 38. Leonardo never seems to have held strong political or personal allegiances, and the milieu of the Sforza court in Milan – whose relationship with Florence was never easy – may well have encouraged such an image.[8]

Finally, one of the versions of the old woman seems to have been known to John Tenniel, and was used by him as the basis for the Ugly Duchess in his illustrations to Lewis Carroll's *Alice's Adventures in Wonderland*, published in 1865 (FIG. 24).

FIG. 24
BROTHERS DALZIEL, after John Tenniel (1820–1914)
Illustration to Lewis Carroll, *Alice's Adventures in Wonderland*, London 1865
Wood engraving, 7.3 × 8.9 cm (2⅞ × 3½″)

1. Erasmus 1979, pp. 48–9.
2. Tietze-Conrat (1957, p. 19) proposed that the drawing was a portrait of a dwarf at the court of Ludovico Sforza; Wasserman (1974, pp. 112f.) went further, suggesting that many of Leonardo's grotesques may have been records of 'an absurd reality Leonardo had found ready-made in Lodovico Sforza's court.'
3. Silver 1984, no. 32A. A variant on the figure, more human and haggard in the features but close in dress, is found in Massys's *Temptation of St Anthony* in the Prado, Madrid (Silver 1984, no. 26). She also appears in an engraving by Hans Liefrinck (Muylle 1994, fig. 1), and in a French religious broadsheet of the 1560s (Lugano 1998, p. 20). For possible routes of transmission of Leonardo's drawings to the north, see Bialostocki 1955 and 1959; Bora in Milan 1982b, pp. 170f.; Cogliati Arano in Milan 1987–8, pp. 28–33; Traversi 1997; Meijer 1998.
4. Private collection, New York. See Silver 1977; Silver 1984, no. 32B.
5. Pennington 1982, no. 1603.
6. Panofsky 1953, pp. 354f.
7. Paris, Musée Jacquemart-André; Silver 1984, no. 54.
8. As suggested by Silver 1977, p. 73.

40

LEONARDO DA VINCI

A satire on aged lovers, c.1490

Black chalk underdrawing, pen and ink
26.2 × 12.3 cm (10⁵⁄₁₆ × 4¹³⁄₁₆″), the top left corner cut
RL 12449

The woman is ridiculously dressed in a tight, low-cut bodice and ostentatious headdress, as seen in CATS. 36 and 39; the gap-toothed man, gazing ardently at her, wears an outsize hat of a type drawn elsewhere by Leonardo (see the centre-left head in CAT. 37). The pale ink and sketchiness of the drawing makes the actions of the figures hard to read, but close examination of the original seems to show that the man is offering the woman a flower, the circular bloom of which is visible above the line of his shoulder. She raises her hand either to decline the flower or to take it between her fingers.[1] The offering of flowers was a standard token of love in Renaissance art (as now), and the drawing is therefore a rather cruel satire on the vanity and ridiculousness of the elderly behaving like young lovers, a theme repeated in the pair of paintings by Massys discussed in CAT. 39.[2]

A common variant on the theme of the foolish lust of the old was that of the ill-matched lovers. Most of these show a young woman filching the purse of a lecherous old man; in a less common variant, an old woman offers money to a scheming youth.[3] A composition of an ill-matched couple apparently originating in a lost drawing by Leonardo was well known in the sixteenth and seventeenth centuries. In this composition a long-haired Leonardesque youth embraces an old woman (with an extravagant coiffure very like Leonardo's *Leda*) while laying his hand on her conspicuous bag of money. The couple were copied in a weak drawing in the Albertina, Vienna, attributed to Joris Hoefnagel[4] and were etched in 1646 by Wenceslaus Hollar with the inscription *Leonardo da Vinci inv.* (FIG. 25), after a prototype then in the Arundel collection along with the drawings now at Windsor.[5] They were also the protagonists of a *Grotesque betrothal* known in several variants of a composition by Quinten Massys or a close follower (FIG. 26), where they were joined by several other figures derived from CAT. 41 and FIG. 22.[6] The association of Leonardo's name with this low-art motif must have been a factor in its popularity and longevity.

FIG. 25
WENCESLAUS HOLLAR (1607–77), after Leonardo(?)
An ill-matched couple, c.1645
Etching, plate 17.0 × 13.1 cm (6¹¹⁄₁₆ × 5³⁄₁₆″)

1. A copy of the drawing of about 1600 in the Albertina, Vienna (inv. 17615), sometimes attributed to Rubens (Jaffé 1966, p. 129) but probably not by that artist, renders the gesture as the man giving a ring to the woman, or taking it from her; the bloom of the flower becomes an indeterminate shape attached to the man's shoulder.

2. It has repeatedly been suggested (e.g. Trutty-Coohill 1997, Pedretti 1997) that the drawing is the missing right half of CAT. 41, a possibility that is ruled out by ink, paper, scale, viewpoint and style.

3. See Coupe 1967, Stewart 1977, and Silver 1984, p. 144, for unequal lovers.

4. Albertina, inv. 348a; Lugano 1998, no. 6. The woman alone is also copied in a drawing in the Louvre, inv. 28781.

5. Pennington 1982, no. 1604. Pedretti (in Keele and Pedretti 1979, II, pp. 858–9) saw on RL 12282v, under a deliberate smudge of ink, lines which he read as a sketch for this composition. I cannot make this out.

6. Silver 1984, p. 144, as a pastiche by a follower of Massys. See also Barryte 1990, reproducing all the above and discussing another print which is just a copy of the Hollar.

41

LEONARDO DA VINCI
A man tricked by Gypsies, c.1493

Pen and ink, 26.0 × 20.5 cm (10¼ × 8¹⁄₁₆″)
RL 12495

This is Leonardo's most complex composition involving the grotesque, and the types depicted can be seen scattered throughout this book.[1] Yet a drawing that so obviously has a narrative subject has usually been explained as simply an assemblage of specimens representing variations on some theme – the humours, physiognomic types, stages of madness, the degenerations of melancholy and so on.[2] The trimming of the sheet at the right has obscured the subject of the drawing, but enough survives to allow the scene to be identified without doubt.

The two figures behind, staring with hooded brow or laughing hysterically, compound the sense of claustrophobic menace, but they are only spectators to the action that takes place between the three characters in the foreground. The central figure holds up his forearm to the old woman on the right, who in turn raises her right hand towards where his hand would be; meanwhile, the crone on the left reaches under the sleeve of the central figure. This is a familiar subject in paintings of more than a century later: the surrounding figures are Gypsies, and the woman on the right reads the palm of the man in the centre while her accomplice steals his purse.

Gypsies had arrived in western Europe from the Balkans in the early fifteenth century, travelling often in large groups with an impressively titled leader, such as Duke of Little Egypt. They carried imperial or papal safe-conducts (usually forged) and claimed to be penitents from Egypt, making a seven-year pilgrimage around Europe to expiate the sin of their forebears who had failed to give succour to the Holy Family. As pilgrims the Gypsies could expect hospitality, but frequently they outstayed their welcome and were moved on by the authorities. Chroniclers record the fascination with which they were regarded by the townspeople, and they soon acquired a reputation for two activities which have remained a stereotype of Gypsy behaviour to this day – fortune-telling and theft. In Paris in 1427, for instance, it was reported that:

In spite of their poverty they had sorceresses among them who looked at people's hands and told them what had happened to them or what would happen. They brought trouble into many marriages, for they would say to the husband, 'Your wife has cuckolded you', or to the wife, 'Your husband has deceived you'. What was worse, it was said that when they talked to people they contrived – either by magic arts or by other means, by the devil's help or by their own skill and cunning – to make money flow out of other people's purses into their own. I must say I went there three or four times to talk to them and could never see that I lost a penny, nor did I see them looking into other people's hands, but everyone said they did.[3]

Gypsies do not appear in Western art until around 1480, and then infrequently. Leonardo himself noted a Gypsy among a list of his drawings compiled in the early 1480s, though this drawing cannot now be identified.[4] Here he depicted the woman on the left in a fringed, tightly knotted headdress (still familiar in seaside fortune-telling booths) and the palmist wrapped in a blanket-like cloak, both reported to be standard Gypsy dress at the time.

The style both of the drawing and of the handwriting of an inscription on the verso dates Leonardo's drawing to the first half of the 1490s. This coincides with a period of growing hostility to Gypsies in Milan, culminating in their banishment from the Duchy, the first such edict in Italy. On 13 April 1493 it was ordered that 'all Gypsies that are presently to be found in these parts must leave immediately and henceforth not venture to return between the Po and the Adda, on pain of the gallows', on the grounds that they had become too numerous and were behaving like 'bandits, ruffians and charlatans', committing thefts and other crimes.[5]

It is doubtful that Leonardo was responsible for inventing the pictorial combination of palmistry and

pickpocketing. The account quoted above shows that the link was well established in popular lore seventy years before Leonardo's drawing, and the motif can be found in several works of around 1500 from across Europe.[6] Pictorially the scene may have been derived from analogous depictions of ill-matched lovers (see CAT. 40), which appear in northern art around this date and also show purse-stealing while the dupe is distracted.

Leonardo may even have fallen victim to such a stratagem himself. While he claimed not to believe in palmistry – he stated 'false physiognomy and chiromancy I will not consider because there is no truth in them as is shown by the way in which such chimeras have no scientific foundation'[7] – he did own one book on the subject by the early 1490s and two by the following decade,[8] and in a list of household expenses of around 1505 he noted six *soldi* 'for telling a fortune'.[9] It would have been quite in character for the endlessly curious artist to have sought out a Gypsy fortune-teller in Milan; and perhaps, therefore, the occasional speculation that the central figure is at some level a likeness of Leonardo may be true in a narrative (rather than representational) sense.

Only the oak wreath worn by the central figure remains mysterious. The oak had several connotations in antiquity and the Renaissance, including hospitality (because of its enveloping foliage), which might explain its presence here – the Gypsies well received by the central figure but abusing his hospitality – but there seems to have been no visual tradition for this.[10] Perhaps Leonardo's intention was simply to render the old man more dignified, effecting a still greater bathetic contrast with the perfidious Gypsies.

Leonardo's composition soon became widely known both in Italy and in the Low Countries, no doubt through the agency of copies. Neither of the two copies that survive shows the act of palmistry, suggesting that the original sheet was trimmed at an early date; the identity of the figures as Gypsies disappeared, and they became merely exemplars of ugliness. Quinten Massys in Antwerp used the heads of the two principal

FIG. 26
Attributed to QUINTEN MASSYS (1465/6–1530)
A grotesque betrothal, c.1520
Oil on panel, 54 × 89 cm (21¼ × 35″)
São Paulo, Museu de Arte

Gypsies as tormentors in his *Martyrdom of St John the Evangelist* (1508–11; Antwerp, Koninklijk Museum), and they were joined by the hysterically laughing figure as three of the spectators to his *Grotesque betrothal* (FIG. 26). It is also possible that Albrecht Dürer knew the composition, and that this knowledge is reflected in his *Christ among the Doctors* (Madrid, Thyssen Collection), painted in Venice in 1506.[11] But half-length multi-figure compositions contrasting a beautiful Christ with ugly tormentors were common throughout Europe by this time, and in surrounding a still centre with impassioned figures (also seen in the *Adoration of the Magi* and the *Last Supper*), Leonardo was following rather than establishing a tradition.

The most significant adaptation of the composition seems to have been Giorgione's use of the central and right-hand figures for his enigmatic profile of a soldier with a leering background figure, in the Kunsthistorisches Museum, Vienna (FIG. 27). The secondary figure lays his or her hand on the soldier's arm, a generalised echo of the palmistry of Leonardo's drawing. Giorgione may have known and retained some of the meaning of Leonardo's drawing, for the soldier was a common symbol of man subject to the vicissitudes of fortune; if the background figure can be read as a Gypsy, already stereotyped in Italy as a fortune-teller and thus, by extension, an embodiment of fortune, the gesture would signify fortune laying its hand on the destiny of the soldier.

FIG. 27
GIORGIONE (*c*.1477/8–1510)
An allegorical portrait of a soldier with a Gypsy (?), *c*.1505–10
Oil on canvas, 72 × 56.5 cm (28½ × 22¼″)
Vienna, Kunsthistorisches Museum

1. This catalogue entry is a condensed version of Clayton 2002.
2. See for instance Suida 1929, p. 100; Richter 1939, II, p. 260; Vallese 1992; Kwakkelstein 1994, p. 76.
3. Shirley 1968, pp. 216–19.
4. Codex Atlanticus, f. 324; Richter 1939, no. 680.
5. Arlati 1989, p. 4.
6. For a good survey of early examples see Cuzin 1977.
7. Codex Urbinas, f. 109r-v.
8. *De chiroma[n]tia* is included in his book list of *c*.1492 (Richter 1939, no. 1469). In the list of *c*.1503–4 (Madrid MS II, ff. 2v-3r) are *de chiromantia* and *de chiromantia da Milano*. Reti (1968) suggested that these might have been *Chiromantia. Ex divina philosophorum academia collecta* (Venice, *c*.1480) and/or *Chyromantica. Scientia naturalis* (Padua, 1484), though they might equally have been unpublished manuscripts.
9. Codex Atlanticus, f. 319v-b; Richter 1939, no. 1534.
10. Levi d'Ancona 1977, pp. 250–5; Cattabiani 1996, pp. 49–60.
11. See primarily Bialostocki 1959.

PORTRAITS

Five painted portraits by Leonardo survive: *Ginevra de' Benci* (Washington), an unidentified *Musician* (Milan, Ambrosiana), *Cecilia Gallerani* (Krakow; FIG. 30), *La Belle Ferronière*, and *Mona Lisa* (both Louvre). We also have a number of portrait drawings by Leonardo, ranging from a full-scale cartoon for an unexecuted painting of Isabella d'Este (FIG. 28) to the briefest small sketches of his acquaintances (FIG. 29).

While Leonardo generally preferred to draw the head in profile, none of his five surviving painted portraits is of this form. Painted portraits were subject to fashion and a patron's wishes in a way that Leonardo's drawings were not. The painted profile had been obsolete in northern Europe for most of the fifteenth century; in Italy the profile lasted longer, and the shift from profile to three-quarters view took a little longer in the portraiture of women than in that of men, but the time-lag is not as marked as has sometimes been claimed, and was driven by aesthetics rather than by a change in the status of women.[1] Towards 1500 the profile was becoming increasingly confined to portraits of the ruling class, and Leonardo's only full-scale portrait in profile is the cartoon of the Duchess of Mantua, Isabella d'Este (FIG. 28). It is notable that Leonardo appears not to have painted the likeness of Ludovico Sforza, even though he was in his employ for a decade and a half; all Ludovico's surviving portraits are in profile, and he preferred to use Leonardo's talents for more demanding portrait formats – the lively allegorical portrait of his mistress Cecilia Gallerani, or the bronze equestrian monument to his father Francesco.

The split between the drawn profile and the painted three-quarters view in Leonardo's portraits was also due to the respective natures of drawing and painting. The line of the drawn profile, with only a little elaboration around the eyes, renders a likeness powerfully and succinctly, but it gives little sense of engagement between the sitter and the viewer. These two qualities, of aloofness and simplified recognisability, made the profile ideal for portraits of rulers; but Leonardo had higher ambitions for his painted portraits, and while these aims became fully articulated only as he began to put together thoughts for his treatise on painting in the

later 1480s, they are implicit in his first surviving portrait, *Ginevra de' Benci* of the mid-1470s. He wished to capture something of the inner nature of the sitter, not just the topography of the face, and this could not be attempted in a profile format. Ginevra's is one of the first Florentine portraits of a woman in three-quarters view (though absolute precedence is impossible to establish), and in this and in its cool tones and meticulous handling the portrait is strongly influenced by Flemish works, of which there were a significant number in Florence.

The character of Leonardo's next surviving portrait, the *Musician* of *c*.1485–8, is probably explained as a response to the work of Antonello da Messina, which Leonardo may not have encountered until he moved to Milan in the early 1480s. The itinerant Antonello combined sophistication of surface with an insistent sense of physical structure to a degree that would have appealed strongly to Leonardo. A painting by Antonello seems to have been acquired by Galeazzo Maria and Ludovico Sforza in 1476 and would presumably have been accessible to Leonardo when he entered Sforza service sometime in the 1480s.[2] The *Musician* is the least personal of Leonardo's painted portraits, with a surface comparable in hardness to the skull drawings of 1489 (CAT. 5) and approaching the dispassionate objectivity of the profile drawings that Leonardo executed in the same decade (CATS. 42, 43).

In Leonardo's next two portraits, the *Lady with an ermine (Cecilia Gallerani)* of *c*.1490 (FIG. 30) and the so-called *Belle Ferronière* of *c*.1495, he struck a perfect balance between the representation of outward appearance and of character. While our attempts to 'read' personality in Renaissance portraits are mostly misplaced, the expression of inner life was plainly Leonardo's intention in these paintings. This interest becomes dominant in Leonardo's last surviving portrait, the *Mona Lisa*, begun around 1503 and worked on over several years. But paradoxically, while it seems to be the most psychologically rich of Leonardo's portraits, the *Mona Lisa* tells us almost nothing about the sitter. It is instead an expression of Leonardo's concerns with the flux of life and the form of the material

world, and the features approach those of Leonardo's late ideal of beauty so closely that it may be questioned to what degree the painting depicts the actual likeness of an individual.[3] The amusing suggestion that the *Mona Lisa* is a self-portrait of Leonardo in women's clothing is of course absurd at a literal level, but does capture a truth about the painting, that the form of the sitter is fundamentally a vehicle for the artist's deepest emotions.

FIG. 28

LEONARDO DA VINCI
A portrait cartoon of Isabella d'Este, 1500
Black, red and yellow chalks, the outlines pricked
63 × 46 cm (24¾ × 18″)
Paris, Musée du Louvre, inv. MI 753

1. See e.g. Simons 1988; Campbell 1990, p. 81;
    Woods-Marsden 2001–2, pp. 69–77.
2. See Marani 2000, p. 200, n. 23.
3. Brown 1983; Hemsoll 1998, p. 73. On the identification of
    the sitter see Shell and Sironi 1991, Zöllner 1993.

42

LEONARDO DA VINCI
A portrait of a man in left profile, c.1480–85

Metalpoint on pale buff prepared paper, 12.7 × 10.6 cm (5 × 4³⁄₁₆″)
Numbered by Melzi .50.
RL 12498

The metalpoint may have faded somewhat, and the drawing is thus rather faint; the portrait also has to compete both with a rather crudely drawn thigh at lower right and with the unusually prominent texture of the paper, which can be read as all manner of distracting arabesques. The delicacy of modelling and the quality of light in the eyes are rather compromised by the emphatic outline, though there is no reason to suppose that this was strengthened by a later hand. Leonardo's wish to fix the profile in such a disconcerting manner, at the expense of the overall effect of the drawing, suggests that it was preparatory for some other work, presumably a small painting. The drawing was probably executed around the time of Leonardo's move from Florence to Milan in the early 1480s; beyond the *Virgin of the Rocks* we know little about Leonardo's work in the early to mid-1480s, and he may well have been responsible for more than the three Milanese portraits that survive today.

There is no external evidence for the identity of the sitter. Wilhelm Valentiner surmised that 'the small, round drawn-in chin ... bespeaks a person who expressed himself in a field remote from reality ... the eye [is that] of a man of high intellect, perhaps of a great artist, for its observing quality is most definite,' and thus proposed that this was a portrait of the artist Antonio Pollaiuolo – a charmingly old-fashioned piece of physiognomical reasoning.[1] A comparison with the authentic likenesses of Pollaiuolo does not discount this hypothesis, but neither is the similarity compelling. The profile resembles rather more closely that of Galeazzo Maria Sforza, the elder brother of Ludovico. Galeazzo was assassinated (aged 32) in 1476, at least five years before Leonardo arrived in Milan, and thus the probability that the drawing was done from the life, and the apparent age of the sitter, would rule out this identification. The distinctively large nose was, however, a family trait of the Sforza and the sitter may have been another member of the family.

1. Valentiner 1937, p. 18.

43

LEONARDO DA VINCI

A portrait of a young woman in right profile,
*c.*1485–90

Metalpoint on very pale buff prepared paper
31.8 × 19.9 cm (12½ × 7¹³/₁₆″), a strip cut from halfway
down the left side
Numbered by Melzi *.14.*
RL 12505

The portrait was drawn directly from the life, and the
very loose exploratory lines, clearly seen around the
chin and nose, are some way from the final form of the
profile. There is a remarkably wide range of handling
of the metalpoint, from the free sweeping outlines of
the bust to the flowing layers of loose hair, to the very
restrained modelling of the face itself. The cheek is
hardly touched, but the small patches of shading at the
eye, nose and chin are so sensitively modulated that
they articulate the entire form. The eye in particular is
masterly: Leonardo has captured both its moistness
and the complex refractions in the cornea that cause
the near side of the iris to disappear and seem to bring
the pupil and the far side of the iris towards the spec-
tator.

Kenneth Clark astutely noted of this drawing that
'admirers of Leonardo, who wish to make all his works
emphatically Leonardesque, should notice how objective his finest work can be.'¹ This objectivity makes the
date of the drawing difficult to determine on stylistic
grounds alone, though the authority with which the
metalpoint is handled probably places it in the mid-to-
late 1480s. It is in any case one of the earliest examples
of what was to become Leonardo's favourite pose, the
bust in three-quarters view with the head in strict
profile.

Attempts have of course been made to connect the
drawing with other works, but it was probably not a
study for a more developed portrait.² While not all portraits of women of the fifteenth century show the sitter

FIG. 29
LEONARDO DA VINCI
*A caricature of a young woman, c.*1485–8
Pen and ink, area shown 11.2 × 7 cm (4⁷/₁₆ × 2⅞″)
Milan, Biblioteca Ambrosiana,
Codex Atlanticus f. 320v-b (detail)

in opulent attire – Leonardo's *Ginevra de' Benci* is dressed
quite plainly – the sitter here is in determinedly every-
day clothing and was probably no more than a plebeian
acquaintance of Leonardo. Only the upper classes
were painted at this time, but Leonardo undoubtedly
sketched the unexceptional figures of his daily life
throughout his career. A young woman as unassuming
as the present sitter was drawn repeatedly on CAT. 1;
and on a miscellaneous sheet in the Codex Atlanticus
(FIG. 29) of about the same date is a small profile of a
young woman with a receding chin and her hair hanging down over her eyes, clearly intended to be an
amusing sketch of an acquaintance.

1. Clark and Pedretti 1968–9, I, p. 88.
2. Wasserman (1974, p. 113) first suggested that the famous
    study of hands at Windsor (FIG. 31) may have been drawn
    from the same sitter, an argument amplified by Colenbrander
    (1992). The connection is seductive, but a collage of the hands
    and the profile demonstrates that the angle at which the

forearms are drawn results in a too-short left upper arm and
a too-long right, and that the torso is curiously distended if
sufficient space is allowed for the left arm. Leonardo could
of course have adjusted the angle of view of the hands in a
subsequent work, but this renders the connection between
the profile and the hands purely speculative.

44

LEONARDO DA VINCI
*Sketches of the head and shoulders of a woman, c.*1490

Metalpoint on pale pinkish-buff prepared paper
23.2 × 19.0 cm (9⅛ × 7½″)
Numbered by Melzi at centre right *49*.
RL 12513

Leonardo drew his model in two basic positions, from the front with the bust turned to the left, and from behind looking over her left shoulder. It is possible to reconstruct with a fair amount of certainty the order in which Leonardo filled his page: six large studies from the front were drawn in the upper half of the sheet, after which the model turned around to be drawn three times towards the bottom of the sheet, twice more in the gaps at the centre of the sheet, and another three times along the top edge. Finally, the model turned back to the front, and Leonardo sketched her twice along the lower edge and twice more up the left edge.

The drawing has usually been assigned to Leonardo's early, Florentine years, but it seems to be significantly later. The handling of the metalpoint, a combination of strong sharp outlines and rapid (but not messy) zig-zag hatching, is that of Leonardo's life studies of horses for the Sforza monument, of around 1490. Further, the distinctive paper (with widely spaced chain lines, very clear laid lines, and prominent diagonal overstitch marks along the chain lines) and the preparation appear to be identical to those of one such study (RL 12317). This dating coincides with that of Leonardo's portrait of *A Lady with an ermine* (FIG. 30), which almost certainly depicts Cecilia Gallerani.[1] Between 1489 and early 1491 Cecilia was the mistress of Ludovico Sforza, and the ermine has several potential meanings: a play on Cecilia's surname (the animal is γαλεη, *galée*, in Greek); an emblem of purity (the ermine would rather die at the hands of a hunter than sully itself in a muddy lair); a talismanic symbol of pregnancy, for in May 1491 Cecilia gave birth to Ludovico Sforza's son, Cesare;[2] and a reference to Ludovico himself, who had been created a member of the Order of the Ermine by the Aragonese King of Naples in 1488. A contemporary poem by Bernardo Bellincioni celebrated a portrait of Cecilia by Leonardo, most probably the Krakow painting (though

FIG. 30
LEONARDO DA VINCI
*A lady with an ermine (Cecilia Gallerani), c.*1490
Oil on panel, 54.8 × 40.3 cm (21⁹/₁₆ × 15⅞″)
Krakow, Museo Czartoryski

Bellincioni does not mention an ermine), and implied the patronage of Ludovico, thus rendering a date *c.*1490 almost certain.

It is thus possible that the present sheet was preparatory for the portrait of Cecilia; the final sketch at centre left corresponds, so far as it goes, exactly with the painting. The pose of Cecilia is highly unconventional – she and her ermine are caught in a moment, reacting to an event beyond the picture frame, and this sense of instantaneity is exactly what Leonardo was searching for in the drawing. The model need not look like Cecilia, for it has always been common practice among portraitists to use a substitute model for studying the pose, and to refer to the actual subject of the portrait only for those elements that require a likeness, often no more than the face.

Given the prominence of the hands in Cecilia's portrait it is likely that Leonardo had been contemplating

FIG. 31
LEONARDO DA VINCI
A study of hands, c.1490
Metalpoint with white heightening, over
charcoal, on pale pink-buff prepared paper
21.5 × 15.0 cm (8⁷⁄₁₆ × 5⁷⁄₈″)
RL 12558

their role from the outset – the sketch to the lower right of centre here shows the model with her left arm akimbo, and that at centre right with her arms folded across her breast. It is thus possible that the famous drawing of hands at Windsor (FIG. 31) was also preparatory for the portrait, for although they do not correspond in pose, they are identical in type – long, bony and elegant; they are drawn in the same style on the same paper with the same preparation as the present sheet, and they must therefore also be dated to around 1490. Again this is much later than usual, as the hands have often been related to the cut-down portrait of Ginevra de' Benci in Washington, painted in the mid-1470s.[3] But if it is accepted that Leonardo could rethink the form of a portrait from his first conception, introducing the prominent and novel device of the ermine

only after some thought, it seems quite plausible that FIG. 31 reflects an early stage in the development of the portrait of Cecilia Gallerani.

1. For the painting see most fully Rome 1998–9.
2. Moczulska 1995; Musacchio 2001.
3. See most recently Washington 2001–2, pp. 142–9. The same redating must also apply to a sheet of studies of an infant, RL 12569, likewise identical in style, paper and preparation. This incidentally solves the problem of RL 12568, a very similarly conceived sheet of studies of an infant in red chalk. While 12569 was thought to be Florentine, it was impossible to resolve the dating of 12568, a sheet with motifs apparently of the 1470s in a medium that Leonardo did not begin to use until the 1490s. Dating both 12568 and 12569 to c.1490 would dispose of this dilemma and confirm 12568 as one of Leonardo's earliest surviving drawings in red chalk.

45

LEONARDO DA VINCI and pupil
The head and shoulders of a woman,
*almost left profile, c.*1485–90

Metalpoint on pale blue prepared paper
16.2 × 12.2 cm (6⅜ × 4¹³⁄₁₆″), top corners trimmed
RL 12512

The drawing appears to be the work of two different hands. The hatching throughout the head is done with the right hand, whereas the few small areas of shading in the bust are done with the left; and the handling there and around the back of the head is so free and assured, and so similar to the equivalent areas of CAT. 43 that the basic outlines must have been drawn by Leonardo. The face, by contrast, is very closely worked and the outline deadened by over-emphasis; it seems too small in relation to the head, and the features sit a little too far forwards and not quite square on the head, like a mask. It is, therefore, probable that the outlines of a model were sketched by Leonardo, and the face worked up by a pupil as a drawing exercise.

The style and technique date the drawing to the later 1480s. The combination of fine shading and the over-emphasis of outlines and facial details is typical of several artists in Leonardo's circle in late fifteenth-century Milan, such as Ambrogio de' Predis and Francesco Napoletano; the style of the present drawing seems to approach most closely that of Giovanni Antonio Boltraffio.[1] What began as a vital drawing by Leonardo from a model was sapped of life by his pupil's assiduousness in pursuing perfection. The features are made to conform to a type of beauty explored by Leonardo in drawings such as that in the Biblioteca Reale, Turin, of the angel for the *Virgin of the Rocks*;[2] but it was primarily the followers of Leonardo who, in drawings like this, created the frozen Leonardesque type that was to be for centuries afterwards regarded as the epitome of the master's work.

1. The drawing was most recently attributed to Boltraffio in Marani 2000, p. 180, but rejected as his in Fiorio 2000, p. 204.
2. Popham 1946, no. 157.

46

Attributed to FRANCESCO MELZI (1491/3–c.1570)

A portrait of Leonardo in profile, c.1515–18

Red chalk
27.5 × 19.0 cm (10¹³⁄₁₆ × 7½″), corners cut
Inscribed below LEONARDO/VINCI
RL 12726

Although not by Leonardo, this drawing is of high quality and is the most objective and accurate portrait of the master to survive. Only one other drawing may with some confidence be taken as a true likeness of Leonardo, a sketch by a pupil on a late sheet of studies showing the artist at about the same age (FIG. 32).[1] The present portrait was most probably executed from the life by Leonardo's pupil Francesco Melzi, though the chalk is more richly handled and varied in its textures than in the copy drawings usually attributed to Melzi (such as CATS. 37–9); there may even be some enlivening strokes by Leonardo himself in the lower part of the hair.[2]

All early writers on Leonardo were agreed that he was beautiful (even if none had known him personally), and that this was a natural, god-given corollary of his personal qualities and his abilities as an artist. The increasingly explicit concept during the sixteenth century of the individual as a mutable social construct required authors to attribute grace and elegance to Leonardo, as a necessary condition for the newly elevated social position of the artist: the artisan of a century earlier was now expected to cultivate the ease of deportment and nobility of the ideal courtier described by Baldassare Castiglione.[3]

Of the early authors, only the appendix to the brief biography by the so-called Anonimo Gaddiano gives some detail of Leonardo's appearance, describing him as having 'a beautiful head of hair down to the middle of his breast, in ringlets and well arranged'.[4] There is, however, no evidence that Leonardo was bearded until his last years. Before the sixteenth century a beard would have been seen as odd on an Italian: they were the preserve of the barbarous, Germans, orientals, figures from ancient history, mythology and biblical times, philosophers, hermits and penitents. Pope Julius II grew a beard in 1510 in remorse for the French invasion of Italy, but it seems to have been Francis I

LEONARDO
VINCI

who from his accession to the throne of France in 1515 sparked the pan-European fashion for beards that endured throughout the sixteenth century.

Unusually for a drawing from the Melzi/Leoni collection, the sheet has been shaped for mounting, the paper has discoloured from exposure to light, and the reverse of the sheet shows signs of having been attached to a support, lifted and restored at an early date. It was presumably framed and hung as a memento of the master, and may well have been the portrait seen by Giorgio Vasari in Melzi's villa many years later: 'Francesco cherishes and preserves these papers as relics of Leonardo, together with the portrait of that artist of such happy memory.'[5]

It was possibly through Vasari's acquaintance with this drawing in the Villa Melzi that the profile frontispiece to the biography of Leonardo in his *Lives of the Artists* (FIG. 33) took the form that it did; and from Vasari's illustration stemmed posterity's image of Leonardo. Intriguingly, the standard type of Aristotle converged with this likeness of Leonardo during the sixteenth century, to become the accepted pattern for the venerable natural philosopher.[6] This fitted so perfectly the popular perception of Leonardo's character before the twentieth century that a now-famous drawing in the Biblioteca Reale, Turin (FIG. 34), was unquestioningly accepted as a self-portrait of Leonardo when it surfaced in the early nineteenth century. That old man with furrowed brow and long beard, gazing into the distance, soon passed into common currency as the definitive likeness of Leonardo and will doubtless retain this status. It has, however, been pointed out that the drawing is a work of the 1490s, when Leonardo was in his mid-forties, and cannot possibly be a self-portrait.[7]

FIG. 32 (*left, above*)
WORKSHOP OF LEONARDO
A sketch of Leonardo, c.1517–18
Pen and ink, area shown 12.5 × 10.0 cm (4¹⁵⁄₁₆ × 3¹⁵⁄₁₆″)
RL 12300v (detail)

FIG. 33 (*left, below*)
After GIORGIO VASARI (1511–74)
Leonardo flanked by personifications of the Arts,
plate to *Delle vite de' piu eccellenti pittori, scultori et architettori,* Florence 1568
Woodcut, image 12.5 × 10.7 cm (4¹⁵⁄₁₆ × 4³⁄₁₆″)

FIG. 34

LEONARDO DA VINCI

The head of an old man, c.1495

Red chalk, 33.3 × 21.3 cm (13⅛ × 8⅜″)

Turin, Biblioteca Reale, inv. 15571

1. Many attempts have been made to identify Leonardo's features in the products of Andrea del Verrocchio's workshop in the 1470s, particularly the bronze *David* (Florence, Museo Nazionale del Bargello). It is true that the profile of the *David* is very like that here, but given the forty-year gap between the two works, the romantic conclusion that the young Leonardo was Verrocchio's model is probably unsupportable. See Brown 1998, p. 8.

2. A copy of the drawing in the Biblioteca Ambrosiana, Milan (repr. Pedretti 1983–6, p. 134) is probably also by Melzi after his own original.

3. See, for example, Greenblatt 1980; Rubin 1990; Rogers 1998.

4. 'Haveva sino al mezzo il petto una bella capellaia et inanellata et ben composta': 'capellaia' in this passage is usually translated as 'beard', given that it reached the middle of Leonardo's breast, but it surely meant his hair. See Vertova 1992 on Leonardo's beard, suggesting that he grew the beard during his illness in Rome, *c.*1515.

5. Vasari 1965, p. 265

6. Planiscig 1927.

7. A dating in the early 1490s was apparently first proposed by Bodmer (1931, p. 398), and was recently restated by Brown (1994, pp. 76–8). Ost (1980) even claimed the Turin portrait to be a forgery by Giuseppe Bossi, though this cannot be justified. For the later depictions of Leonardo in general see Vinci 1997.

EXPRESSION

Leonardo held that 'the good painter has two principal things to paint: that is, man and the intention of his mind. The first is easy, the second difficult, because it has to be represented by gestures and movements of the parts of the body.'[1] The aim was to involve the viewer by inducing the same emotions as those shown by the figures depicted. The problem came in attempting to codify the expressions, gestures or postures: the recommendations were either too general to be useful, or so specific that following them would have resulted in a mechanical and repetitive composition. It is notable that, although most theoreticians on the arts (including Leonardo) followed Leon Battista Alberti's *On Painting* of 1435 in asserting that a work 'will move spectators when the men painted in the picture outwardly demonstrate their own feelings as clearly as possible,'[2] few before the seventeenth century dealt with the subject in any detail.[3]

The first outline of Leonardo's intended treatise on anatomy, *c.*1489–90, envisaged illustrations of

> the four universal conditions of man, that is, joy with different ways of laughing, and draw the causes of the laughter; weeping in different ways, with their cause; fighting, with the different movements of killing; flight, fear, ferocity, boldness, murder, and everything belonging to such events.[4]

Such things were, of course, more appropriate to a treatise on painting than one on anatomy, and Leonardo's subsequent anatomical researches dealt little with the subject of expression. Cat. 50, drawn almost twenty years after this note, is one of the few sheets to study the movements of the face, and makes no mention of the emotions. Fig. 35, on the reverse of cat. 14 and executed a couple of years later, is a more sophisticated dissection of the facial muscles and identifies two groups of muscles responsible for the most overt signs of emotion. The notes state that:

> *h* [lateral portion of the frontalis, above the eyebrow] is the muscle of anger; *p* [median portion of the frontalis, between the eyebrows] is the muscle of sadness … *ot* [procerus, from the cheekbone to the upper lip] is the muscle of anger …. Note whether the muscle which raises the nares of the horse is the same as that which lies here in man at *f* [i.e. procerus].

These two components of expression, the wrinkling of the brow and the curling of the lips, were treated in Leonardo's notes and drawings almost to the exclusion of all others. Cats. 47–9 show man, horse and lion all displaying anger using the same fundamental facial indicators, and they are dealt with briefly in Leonardo's notes towards his treatise on painting:

> First of laughter and weeping, wherein the mouth, cheeks and closing of the eyes are very similar, and only the eyebrows and interval between them differ …. He who sheds tears raises his eyebrows until they join and draws them together, producing wrinkles in the middle of his forehead, and turns down the corners of his mouth, but he who laughs raises them, and his eyebrows are unfurrowed and apart.[5]

Other discussions of emotion in the treatise have more of the flavour of *ekphrasis*, a literary exercise in the description of a painting:

> You will show the figure of an angry man holding another down on the ground by the hair of his twisted head, his knees on the other's ribs, and his right arm raising his fist on high. His own hair will stand on end, his eyebrows are lowered and drawn together, his teeth are clenched, the corners of his mouth turn down in a curve, his neck is swollen and in front is full of wrinkles because he is bending over his enemy.[6]

This interest in the expression of emotion is reflected much more strongly in Leonardo's paintings than in his drawings, for it is the common aim of his three great compositions, the *Adoration of the Magi*, the *Last Supper* and the *Battle of Anghiari*. By contrast the studies connected with the *Last Supper* (cats. 51–5) give no indication of the intensity of the painting, and few of Leonardo's independent (non-narrative) drawings of

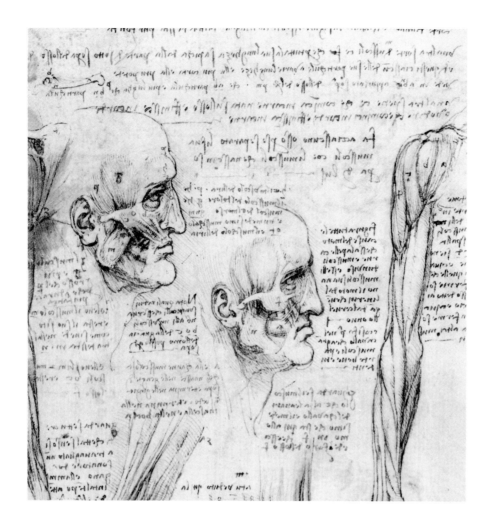

heads show any kind of emotion. The figures in CATS. 40 and 41 leer, cackle or laugh maniacally, but they are participants in narratives; a couple of the small grotesques open their mouths wide in laughter, but this is merely one component of the grotesque effect. There is no study purely of expression by Leonardo like that by a follower of his in the British Museum, showing a youth screwing up his eyes (FIG. 36).

The glut of copies and (more insidiously) pastiches of Leonardo's drawings throughout the sixteenth century led to a distorted perception of the nature of Leonardo's studies of heads, especially in Milan where his memory was most honoured. The *Last Supper* was the only major painting by Leonardo still known to the Milanese, and his independent head studies were thus interpreted in terms of the emotional expression seen in that painting. An anecdote recounted by Gian Paolo Lomazzo in 1584 epitomises the later sixteenth-century understanding of his drawings:

There is a tale told by men of his time, his servants, that Leonardo once wished to make a picture of some laughing peasants (though he did not carry it out but only drew it). He picked out certain men whom he thought appropriate for his purpose and, after getting acquainted with them, arranged a feast for them with some of his friends, and sitting close to them he proceeded to tell them the maddest and most ridiculous tales imaginable, making them, who were unaware of his intentions, laugh uproariously. Whereupon he observed all their gestures very attentively and the ridiculous things they were doing, and impressed them on his mind; and after they had left, he retired to his room and there made a perfect drawing which moved those who looked at it to laughter as if they had been moved by Leonardo's stories at the feast.[7]

FIG. 35 *(left)*
LEONARDO DA VINCI
The anatomy of the face, c.1510–11
Pen and ink with wash, over black chalk
area shown 12.5 × 11.5 cm (4⁵⁄₁₆ × 4½″)
RL 12012v (detail)

FIG. 36
GIOVANNI AGOSTINO DA LODI
(fl. c.1467–c.1502)
A youth screwing up his eyes, c.1520
Red chalk, 25.3 × 18.1 cm (9¹⁵⁄₁₆ × 7⅛″)
London, British Museum, Department of
Prints and Drawings, inv. 1895-9-15-481

This account probably refers to the *Man tricked by Gypsies* (CAT. 41), of whose subject Lomazzo was evidently unaware, and encompasses several of the clichés common in later descriptions of Leonardo's practice – the observation of common people, the memorisation for later recording, the depiction of emotion that moves the viewer to the same response. An apprehension of Leonardo's head drawings as studies of emotion would have been encouraged by an awareness of his notes towards the *Treatise*, which had been transcribed by Francesco Melzi and may well have been circulating in Milan in partial manuscript form. Modern scholars are not immune from this over-interpretation of the head studies: it has recently been proposed that Leonardo actually composed a treatise on the expression of the emotions (*moti mentali*), though the evidence for this in the writings of Lomazzo and of Vicente Carducho, an even later source, is too vague to sustain the thesis.[8]

1. Codex Urbinas, f. 60v; McMahon 1956, no. 248.
2. Alberti 1972, p. 81.
3. See Montagu 1994, pp. 58–67.
4. RL 19037v; Richter 1939, no. 797.
5. Codex Urbinas, ff. 107v, 127r; McMahon 1956, nos 418, 421.
6. Codex Urbinas, f. 126v; McMahon 1956, no. 422.
7. Lomazzo 1584, II, ch. 1; Richter 1939, I, p. 29.
8. Kwakkelstein 1993b; 1994, pp. 63–78.

48

47

LEONARDO DA VINCI

Heads of horses, a lion and a man, c.1503–4

Pen and ink with wash, and a little red chalk
19.6 × 30.8 cm (7¹¹⁄₁₆ × 12⅛″)
RL 12326 (Pedretti 1987, no. 117)

48

LEONARDO DA VINCI

The head of a horse, c.1503–4

Pen and ink with wash, 10.8 × 6.1 cm (4¼ × 2⅜″)
Numbered by Melzi *.89.*
RL 12327 (Pedretti 1987, no. 116)

The two drawings were originally part of the same sheet: a diagram of the sun's orbit around the earth running across the versos of both indicates that CAT. 48 should be placed about 3 centimetres from the lower right edge of CAT. 47. The curved horizontal line to the lower right of CAT. 47, passing through the legs of the rearing horse, is thus the back of the horse on CAT. 48, which was drawn looking backwards over its right shoulder.

The studies were preparatory for the great mural of the *Battle of Anghiari*, in the Sala del Gran Consiglio of the Palazzo della Signoria in Florence. Leonardo agreed to paint the mural some time in mid-1503; the following year, a pendant, the *Battle of Cascina*, was commissioned from his young rival Michelangelo. Work on the *Battle of Anghiari* proceeded with interruptions until in May 1506 Leonardo was called back to Milan, never to return to the project. Only a portion of the centre of the painting, known as the *Fight for the standard*, was completed, and this was widely copied (FIG. 37) before its replacement by Vasari's frescos after 1563.

The *Battle of Anghiari*, more than any other composition of Leonardo's career, gave full rein to his interest in the depiction of powerful emotion. While the passions in the *Last Supper* were intense, decorum

prevented Leonardo from showing the Apostles hurling themselves around the table. But the decorum of a battle scene was extreme rage, and in Leonardo's preparatory drawings he studied the indicators of fury in the faces of man and horse (and, for comparative purposes, a lion). A list of Leonardo's books made around this time includes 'a book of horses sketched for the cartoon'[1] which must have contained many similar drawings.

By contrast to CAT. 22, Leonardo did not wish to suggest that the faces of the different species were similar in appearance; this was a true piece of comparative anatomy, an investigation into the manner in which analogous muscles in each species cause analogous expressions. An earlier note (*c.*1492) on the depiction of the vanquished in battle corresponds closely with these drawings:

> Their brows raised and knit, and the skin above their brows furrowed with pain, the sides of the nose with wrinkles going in an arch from the nostrils to the eyes, the nostrils drawn up ... the lips arched to show the upper teeth, and the teeth apart as if crying out in lamentation.'[2]

Two drawings in the *Szépművészeti Múzeum*, Budapest (FIGS. 38, 39), show the results of Leonardo's research. These carefully worked studies of the heads of warriors in the *Fight for the standard* are among the most satisfying of all of Leonardo's preparatory drawings: he was not tempted into over-elaboration, concentrating on the faces alone and laying out the rest of the heads in a few quick lines. The old soldier is Leonardo's standard type, with the beetling forehead, wrinkled nose and strongly lined open mouth studied in CAT. 47. The young warrior, however, is atypical of Leonardo's heads: the artist knew that his usual youthful profile would appear too delicate in this context, and he rendered him instead as a smooth-skinned version of the old man, with hooded brow and strongly ridged nose but without the creases and folds of a veteran.

1. Madrid MS II, f. 3r.
2. Ashburnham MS II, f. 30v; Richter 1939, no. 602. See also Laurenza 1997, pp. 274–7.

FIG. 37
Attributed to PETER PAUL RUBENS (1577–1640),
after Leonardo
The fight for the standard, c.1600–8
Black chalk, pen and ink, wash, white and grey bodycolour
45.2 × 63.7 cm (17¹³⁄₁₆ × 25¹⁄₁₆″)
Paris, Musée du Louvre, inv. 20271

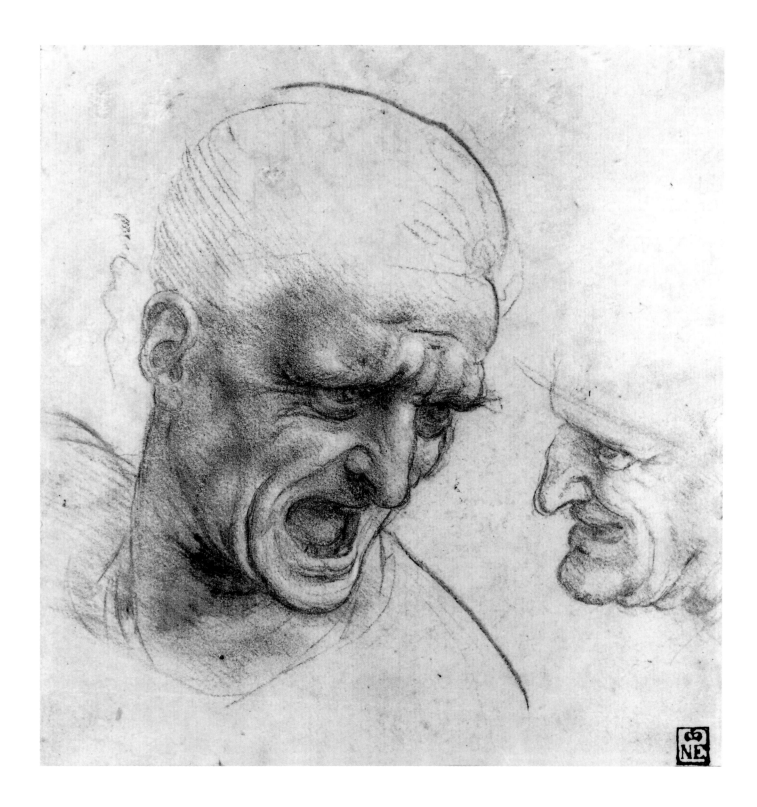

FIG. 38
LEONARDO DA VINCI
Studies of the heads of two warriors, c.1504
Black chalk with touches of red chalk
19.1 × 18.8 cm (7⅛ × 7⅜″)
Budapest, Szépművészeti Múzeum, inv. 1775

FIG. 39 *(right)*
LEONARDO DA VINCI
A study of the head of a young warrior, c.1504
Red chalk, 22.7 × 18.6 cm (8¹⁵⁄₁₆ × 7⁵⁄₁₆″)
Budapest, Szépművészeti Múzeum, inv. 1774

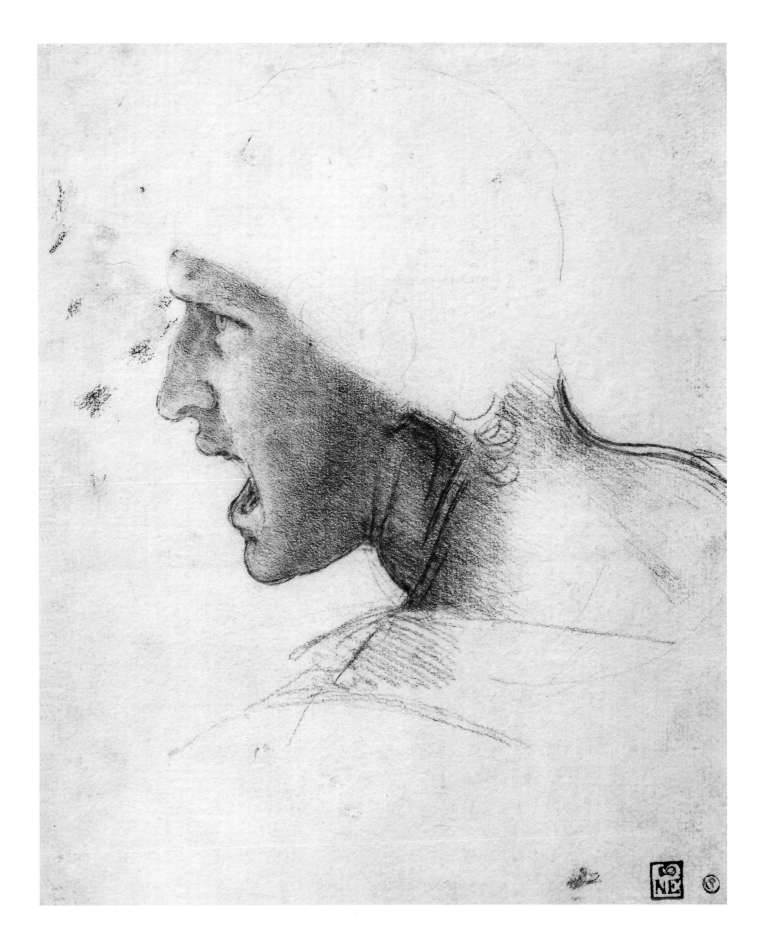

49

LEONARDO DA VINCI
The head of a snarling lion, c.1500–2

Pen and ink and red chalk
8.7 × 6.4 cm (3⁷⁄₁₆ × 2½″), maximum
RL 12587 (Keele and Pedretti 1979, no. 38v)

This intense study of a snarling lion may well have been drawn from the life soon after Leonardo's return to Florence in 1500, for lions – a symbol of the city – were kept in a cage behind the Palazzo della Signoria at this time. The red chalk has suffered badly from rubbing and was originally much stronger; Leonardo may have added the ink later to fix an image quickly sketched on the spot.

The inscription below is unrelated to the lion's head. It is one of Leonardo's puzzle-fables, which are often descriptions of apparent disasters that transpire to refer to the normal lives of animals. Here Leonardo inverts the usual order of his riddles, naming the animals first and so spoiling the surprise:

Of bees. They live together in communities and are destroyed in order to take their honey from them. Many and very great populations will be destroyed in their own dwellings.

50

LEONARDO DA VINCI
The anatomy of the mouth, c.1508

Pen and ink over black chalk
19.2 × 14.2 cm (7⁹⁄₁₆ × 5⁹⁄₁₆″)
RL 19055v (Keele and Pedretti 1979, no. 52v)

The sheet comes from the so-called Anatomical Manuscript B, a notebook that Leonardo began in 1489 with the skull drawings (CAT. 5) and returned to almost twenty years later. This second phase covers a wide range of material – the viscera, veins and arteries, nerves, muscles, the structure of the brain and so on – now based on a degree of dissection (human and animal) as well as surface observation, received wisdom and pure speculation.

Here Leonardo investigates the muscles and sinews responsible for moving the lips and thus changing the expression of the mouth, though he makes no mention of the emotions that might trigger their movements. This should be basic knowledge for the artist, who with a full and scientific understanding of his medium – the human form – would be able to create precisely the effects that he desired.

At the top of the page are illustrated 'the two movements which make the lips close tight' – stretched into a smile or puckered into a pout; Leonardo suggests that 'the ultimate shortening of the mouth is equal to half its greatest extension', an echo of the proportional investigations that dominated his first anatomical campaign. He also notes that '[the muscles] in their pulling are of such power that holding the teeth somewhat apart, they will pull the lips inside the mouth, as is demonstrated in the mouth *gh*'; the accompanying illustration, the cross-section at lower centre, is reminiscent of the profiles of toothless old men drawn by Leonardo throughout his life. To the upper right are three drawings with the lips pulled back, not in an expression of anger as in CATS. 47–9, but to show the frenulum of both upper and lower lip, 'the cause of the mouth closing'. The strange small diagram at centre right is a sketch of the gravid uterus of a cow, the subject of studies on the other side of the sheet.

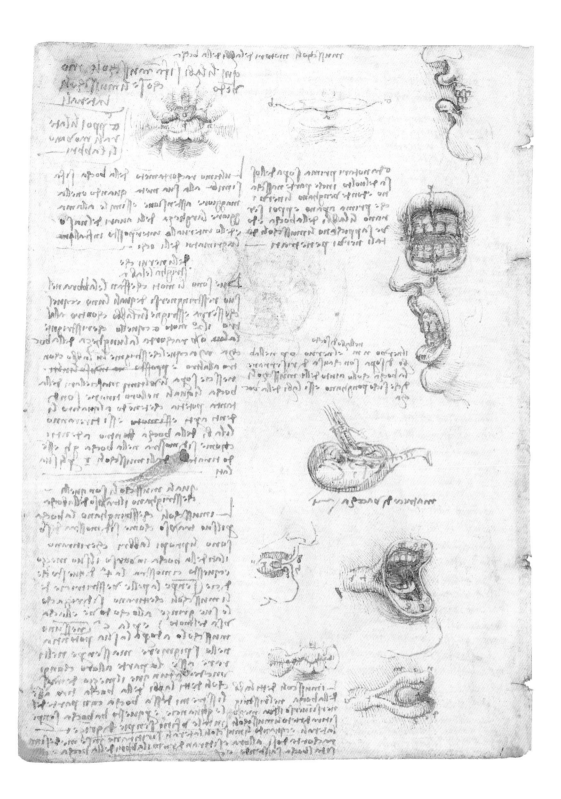

THE LAST SUPPER

Leonardo's greatest painting to reach completion was the *Last Supper*, in the refectory of Santa Maria delle Grazie, Milan (FIG. 40). The monastery church was a focus of Sforza patronage: in 1492 work began on a new tribune designed by the architect Donato Bramante which was later to house the tomb of Ludovico and his wife, and painted lunettes above the *Last Supper* with inscriptions and Sforza coats of arms testify that it, too, was commissioned by the Duke.

Our knowledge of the progress of Leonardo's work on the mural is very patchy. Two compositional sketches can be dated to around 1493; the poet Matteo Bandello claimed to have witnessed Leonardo working concurrently on the clay model for the Sforza monument and on the *Last Supper*, implying that Leonardo began to paint in the refectory before work halted on the Sforza monument, probably in late 1494. A letter of 29 June 1497 from Ludovico Sforza to his secretary asked him to press Leonardo to finish the mural so that the artist could begin work on another wall of the refectory. The dedication to Ludovico Sforza of Luca Pacioli's *De divina proportione*, dated 9 February 1498, speaks of the painting as if it were complete. Leonardo painted the *Last Supper* in an experimental technique combining oil, tempera and varnish, and the mural was already deteriorating within his own lifetime. Countless interventions have culminated in a recent radical cleaning to remove later overpaint, and what we now see is a mere ghost of Leonardo's intentions.[1]

The *Last Supper* is the most overtly cogitated of Leonardo's paintings, with an intensely formal interplay of gestures, sometimes amplifying and sometimes counterbalancing each other. All the hands except one (the left hand of St Thomas) are shown, and most of these have an expressive role: the painting demands that we make a link between these gestures and the workings of the mind. The precise moment depicted has been the subject of much debate, and is perhaps indefinable. Leonardo wished to invest the painting with the full significance of the Last Supper, combining the Institution of the Eucharist with the reaction of the disciples to Christ's announcement of his betrayal, and there is thus no one line in the Gospels to which the mural is exclusively an illustration.

We have some evidence of Leonardo's struggle to obtain the necessary variety of types, for the *Last Supper* is his only work for which we have notes specifically on the composition. A passage in a notebook of *c*.1493–4 lists possible attitudes and reactions of the disciples:

> One who was drinking and has left the glass in its position and turned his head towards the speaker. Another, twisting the fingers of his hands together, turns with stern brow to his companion. Another with his hands spread open shows the palms, and shrugs his shoulders up to his ears, making a mouth of astonishment. Another speaks into his neighbour's ear and he, as he listens to him, turns towards him to lend an ear, while he holds a knife in one hand, and in the other the loaf half cut through by the knife. Another who has turned, holding a knife in his hand, upsets with his hand a glass on the table.

> Another lays his hand on the table and is looking. Another blows his mouth out. Another leans forward to see the speaker, shading his eyes with his hand. Another draws back behind the one who leans forward, and sees the speaker between the wall and the man who is leaning.[2]

This passage is not accompanied by a drawing, and only a few elements correspond with the two surviving compositional drawings and the painting. Indeed it does not sound like a coherent composition; perhaps Leonardo was simply listing possible gestures without at that stage trying to fit them together. The uncharacteristically gauche study for the project in the Accademia, Venice (FIG. 41), gives a similar impression of an assemblage of individual responses, though some of the interactions evident in the painting can be seen in embryo form;[3] the other compositional study (RL 12542), in pen and ink, is much more lucidly conceived but is too sketchy to enable us to read any expression in detail. The chasm in achievement between these drawings and the finished composition hints at Leonardo's efforts to knit the thirteen men together, but these efforts did not have wholly beneficial

FIG. 40
LEONARDO DA VINCI
The Last Supper, c.1495–8
Oil and tempera on plaster, 460 × 880 cm (15′ × 29′2″)
Milan, Santa Maria delle Grazie

consequences, and Kenneth Clark noted that the calculated perfection of the gestures is ultimately discomforting: what should be spontaneous is instead frozen in grandeur.[4]

In large part Leonardo must be excused this effect, for only the forms of the gestures have survived in the painting, and despite the recent cleaning the subtle humanity of the facial expressions is mostly lost. Leonardo was well aware that he had to differentiate the disciples not only in their poses but also facially. He had painted an array of interacting expressive figures fifteen years earlier in the unfinished *Adoration of the Magi*, but the congestion of that composition disguised to some degree the similarities of figure type. With the exception of Joseph and the Magi, the men of the *Adoration* have no specific identity and can merge into a mass of astonished humanity. The *Last Supper*, however, exposed Leonardo to the dangers of monotony. The required format, a line of men at a table, was inherently repetitive, and even if the characters of some of the disciples were indistinct in Scripture, Leonardo could not simply assemble an array of old bearded men and pretty youths as he had in the *Adoration*.

Three expressions are mentioned in the passage quoted above – a stern brow, an astonished shrug, the blowing out of the mouth – but the surviving drawings are primarily studies in facial structure rather than expression. Leonardo seems to have made a very deliberate effort to get away from his stock types, even if several of the faces ultimately approximated to his usual warrior (CAT. 53) or old man (CAT. 54). When Cardinal Luigi of Aragon viewed the *Last Supper* in Milan on 29 December 1517, twenty years after the mural had been completed (and two months after he had visited Leonardo in Amboise), his secretary Antonio de Beatis recorded that 'the figures [in the *Last Supper*] are portraits from the life of eminent Milanese courtiers and citizens of the time.'[5] Two of Leonardo's notes of the period support this statement, identifying potential models: 'Christ: Count Giovanni, the one with the cardinal of Mortaro',[6] and 'Alessandro Carissimo da Parma, for the hand of Christ'.[7] Other possible models, though not necessarily connected with the *Last Supper*, were listed at the same time: 'Cristofano da Castiglione who lives at the Pietà has a fine head,'[8] and (a woman, but testifying to Leonardo's general interest in the faces of individuals) 'Giovannina, fantastic face, is at Santa Caterina, at the hospital.'[9]

FIG. 41
LEONARDO DA VINCI
A study for the Last Supper, c.1493–4
Red chalk, touches of pen and ink
25.9 × 39.4 cm (10³⁄₁₆ × 15½″)
Venice, Galleria dell'Accademia, inv. 254

Leonardo's reputed practice was recounted by Gian-battista Cinthio in 1554:

> Whenever he would paint some figure, he considered first its quality and its nature, whether it was noble or plebeian, happy or severe, troubled or serene, old or young, irritated or tranquil, good or wicked; and then knowing its being, he went where he knew persons of that kind congregated and observed diligently their faces, manner, clothes and bodily movements. Having found that which seemed to him fitting, he drew it with his stylus in the little book that he always kept at his belt. And having done this again and again, and feeling satisfied that he had collected sufficient material for the figure which he wished to paint, he would proceed to give it shape and did it marvellously. Though he did this in all his works, he did it with all diligence in the table he painted in Milan in the convent of the preaching friars, in which is depicted our Redeemer with his disciples at their meal.[10]

Cinthio's account was adopted by Vasari in 1568, and subsequently became a commonplace in discussions of the *Last Supper*. But only one of the surviving drawings for the mural seems to have been done from the life (CAT. 51);[11] the remaining head studies come from a later stage of the creative process, in which Leonardo expunged the quirks of reality so that the features approximated more closely to his standard types. Certainly CATS. 53 and 54 look more like creatures of Leonardo than individuals from the court or streets of Milan; Leonardo was not Caravaggio. Indeed an accusation of vain automimesis (the tendency of an artist to depict figures that resemble himself; see p. 54) in a sonnet by Gaspare Visconti, written in Milan between January 1497 and March 1499, must have been aimed at Leonardo and the *Last Supper*:

There is one nowadays who has so fixed
In his conception the image of himself
That when he wishes to paint someone else
He often paints not the subject but himself.
And not only his face, which is beautifully fair
According to himself, but in his supreme art
He forms with his brush his manners and his
customs ...[12]

After the destruction of the *Battle of Anghiari* in the 1560s, the *Last Supper* became one of the three pillars of Leonardo's reputation for succeeding centuries (the other two being the *Treatise* and the grotesques). Engravings and painted copies of the whole composition were executed from an early date,[13] and it became one of those few paintings (along with Raphael's *Transfiguration* and Michelangelo's *Last Judgement*) of which the details were as famous as the whole. Copies of the heads – individually, in groups and in complete series – circulated throughout Italy and beyond. Some were direct copies from Leonardo's original drawings (CAT. 55), and a few must have been traced from the mural itself, but the majority were copies of copies to the nth degree, and through this process Leonardo's subtleties were gradually debased.

The status of the *Last Supper* as an exemplar of expressiveness, however, remained unchallenged. Its emotional vividness was noted by Pacioli as early as 1498, and subsequent writers attempted to outdo each other in their acclamation of its passions. But while there was a consensus that Leonardo succeeded wonderfully in rendering the mental states of the disciples, there was no general agreement on what those mental states were. The ultimate problem with the depiction of emotion is that unless one resorts to a codification as rigorous (and thus sterile) as that of the academies of the late seventeenth and eighteenth centuries, it is very difficult to represent a facial expression in an unambiguously legible way without the context being wholly provided by the surroundings. We know what emotions are expressed by the heads in CATS. 51–5 because we know the *Last Supper*, and it is far from certain how we would read the drawings if we had lost all knowledge of the composition.

1. For the project see especially Pedretti 1983–6, and most recently Milan 2001.
2. Codex Forster II, ff. 62v–63r; Richter 1939, nos 665–6.
3. The drawing has often been rejected in the past, and even considered to be a forgery (see Milan 2001, no. 41), but is probably authentic: see Venice 1992, p. 232.
4. Clark 1935, p. 100.
5. 'Li personaggi di quello son de naturale retracti de più persone de la Corte et de Milanesi di quel tempo di vera statura'; Pedretti 1983–6, p. 145.
6. Codex Forster II, f. 3r; Richter 1939, no. 667. In the Pinacoteca di Brera (Milan 2001, no. 40) is a large drawing in black and coloured chalks corresponding with the head of Christ, but this is so ruined and reworked that its original status is impossible to judge.
7. Codex Forster II, f. 6r; Richter 1939, no. 1403.
8. Codex Forster III, f. 1v; Richter 1939, no. 1387.
9. Codex Forster II, f. 3r; Richter 1939, no. 1404.
10. Cinthio 1554, p. 193; Richter 1939, I, pp. 28f; Kwakkelstein 1994, pp. 86f., 139.
11. The fragment RL 12466 shows an old bearded man whose facial type is very similar to that of St Andrew, third from the left in the mural; it can be dated to the mid-1490s and may have been sketched by Leonardo in connection with the *Last Supper*, though there is no way of proving this. A metalpoint drawing of a bearded man gesticulating, in the Albertina, Vienna (Popham 1946, no. 164), has also often been associated with the *Last Supper* but has no certain connection with the mural as executed.
12. Visconti 1979, CLXVIII, pp. 117–8, quoted in Kemp 1984–5, p. 199 and Zöllner 1992, p. 147.
13. Milan 1984, pp. 49–100.

51

LEONARDO DA VINCI
*The head of St James, and
architectural sketches, c.*1495

Red chalk, and pen and ink
25.2 × 17.2 cm (9¹⁵⁄₁₆ × 6¾″)
Numbered by Melzi .44.
RL 12552

The drawing is a study for the figure of St James the Greater, second to the right of Christ in the *Last Supper* (FIG. 42). It is markedly different in nature from the other studies for the mural, having the rapidity and variety of finish of a sketch from the life. The red chalk is coarsely handled, as was usual in Leonardo's drawings of the mid-1490s in that medium, and only the eyes and mouth, the principal vehicles of emotion, are heavily worked. The direction of the gaze is not easy to discern – the model could be looking down or glowering out from under a suddenly hooded brow. The left arm is held into the side with the elbow bent and the hand apparently holding something. The angle at which the head is held was carried over to the paint-

ing, where the figure is bearded and holds his arms wide in horror; but the face in the mural is ruined and, as here, it is impossible to be certain whether St James casts his eyes down or stares straight at Christ.

The four architectural sketches seem to have been added after the figure drawing, and confirm the status of the sheet as an informal working study. They are usually described as studies for modifications to the Castello Sforzesco, though there is no firm evidence for this.[1]

---

1. Pedretti (1986, p. 81) suggested tentatively that the sketches may instead have been for the Palazzo Carmagnola, which Ludovico Sforza had given in 1491 to Cecilia Gallerani.

FIG. 42 Detail of FIG. 40

52

LEONARDO DA VINCI
The head of St Philip, c.1495

Black chalk, 19.0 × 15.0 cm (7½ × 5⅞")
Numbered by Melzi .27.

RL 12551

The youth here displays calm, if rapt, contemplation, whereas St Philip in the painting, three to Christ's left, stares towards his master in desperation (FIG. 42). The features of the painted figure are heavier and more fleshy, and he strains forward, pulling taut the skin under his neck. Facially the model resembles CAT. 51, but the apparent similarities should not obscure the different nature of the drawing.[1] The spontaneity of that drawing is replaced here by careful cogitation. There are no corrections; the face is uniformly finished, with a heavily drawn outline, and the eye has a hard quality that suggests it was not drawn from the life. This would appear to be the stage in Leonardo's creative process after the life drawing, when he fixed the image as the basis for subsequent work. The features have already been idealised to a degree, taking the figure one step out of the real world and into the divine.[2]

1. Pedretti (1983–6, pp. 32, 104) suggested that the model here was female, noting a 'string or ribbon that holds the hair'. What appears in reproduction to be a band running across the hair is in fact no more than an old abrasion to the surface of the paper. Marani (2000, p. 96) claimed that the head of St Philip is a mirror image of Leonardo's earlier St Jerome, and that Leonardo may have reused a cartoon. While the emotionality is of a similar order, there is no correspondence between the two.

2. Brown (in Venice 1992, pp. 87ff.) held that this drawing was 'central to understanding Leonardo's importance for Venetian art', and that 'another similar drawing, perhaps, brought to Venice and left there, seems to have become the nucleus of a series of experiments whose goal was to transform Venetian narrative painting.' Puppi (1993, p. 127) was rightly sceptical about the supposed derivations, but they were reiterated and expanded by Brown in Milan 2001, p. 264.

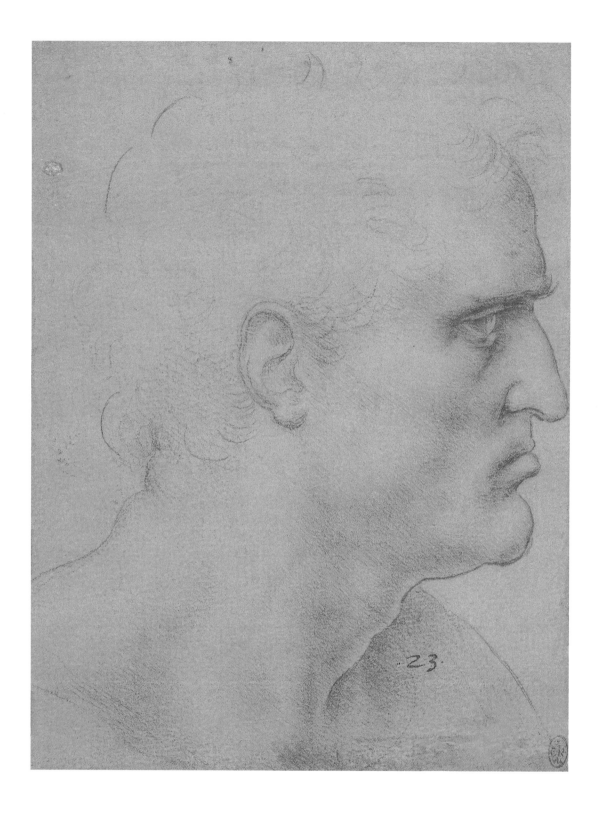

53

LEONARDO DA VINCI
The head of St Bartholomew(?),
*c.*1495 or later

Red chalk on red prepared paper
19.3 × 14.8 cm (7⅝ × 5¹³⁄₁₆″)
Numbered by Melzi *.23.*
RL 12548

The head seems to correspond with that of the disciple at the far left of the *Last Supper* (FIG. 43), generally
thought to be St Bartholomew, though the profile of
that figure is a wreck and the drawing could conceiv-
ably have corresponded more closely with the head of
St Matthew, three from the right. Neither, however,
shares the heaviness of facial feature seen in the drawing, which is closer to Leonardo's standard warrior
type (CAT. 20) than to any of the heads in the *Last Supper*
as painted.

Like the study in the same media for the head of
Judas (CAT. 54), the authenticity of the present sheet
has been doubted, though it has a sound claim to be by
Leonardo himself. The extreme subtlety of modelling,
especially of the complex area around the eye, is of a
wholly different order than a copyist could have
achieved; the handling of the light, reflected on the
profile of the throat and shining through the cornea, is
much more ambitious and accomplished than in the
copy of St Simon (CAT. 55).

If the study of St Philip was one stage further in the
creative process than that of St James, this drawing
seems to be another stage further still. There is no
searching for form: the image has an air of finality, and
it must even be questioned whether the drawing had
any preparatory role in the painting of the *Last Supper*.
The use of red chalk on red prepared paper was one of
Leonardo's favourite techniques in the years after 1500,
but there are surprisingly few non-scientific drawings
by Leonardo datable to the period 1495–1500 that would
allow us to follow his stylistic and technical development at this time. Leonardo's decision not to execute
the mural in fresco – a technique he seems never to
have trained in – obviated the need to work quickly on
successive areas of the composition, and there is no
evidence that he used a cartoon (or cartoons). Having
blocked out the structure of the painting on the wall,
Leonardo may simply have consulted definitive study
drawings by eye while working on the painting,
though there are none of the accidental paint marks
here that might be expected if the sheet had had this
workshop function. Alternatively the drawing may have
been a later 'fair copy' by Leonardo himself, intended
to preserve his invention for future reference and as a
model for his pupils; while there is no evidence that
Leonardo made drawings expressly for this purpose,
the number of copies of the *Last Supper* heads demonstrates that they were certainly used in this way.

FIG. 43 Detail of FIG. 40

54

LEONARDO DA VINCI (with additions?)
*The head of Judas, c.*1495 or later

Red chalk on red prepared paper
18.0 × 15.0 cm (7 $\frac{1}{16}$ × 5 $\frac{7}{8}$ ")
Numbered by Melzi *.33.*
RL 12547

FIG. 44   Detail of FIG. 40

This is one of the few drawings in the whole of Leonardo's oeuvre to present a real problem of attribution. The modelling is handled with great subtlety, but the schematic outlines of the profile are drawn with a lack of modulation that is usually the sign of a copy. The drawing makes a much better impression with the profile covered, and Clark's theory that this is an original study by Leonardo with the outlines subsequently strengthened by a different hand may well be correct.[1] But, like CAT. 53, it is not an exploratory drawing, nor does it correspond particularly closely with the painting (FIG. 44), so far as can be judged. The drawing may again be a definitive record by Leonardo of the final form of the head of Judas, either as the summation of his preparatory work or as a record for posterity.

The drawing shows that Leonardo did not conceive of Judas as facially repulsive, but subsequent copyists of the head and later 'restorers' of the mural itself, encouraged by the literary descriptions of Leonardo's models, exaggerated the stereotypical semitic/criminal features of Judas to an increasingly grotesque degree, hooking his nose down almost to meet his chin. The head in this drawing, by contrast, registers merely mild surprise rather than evil intent. As Clark drily observed, 'this rather pathetic old man is less criminal in appearance than most of the Apostles.'[2]

Gianbattista Cinthio recounted an anecdote about the head of Judas in his book on poetic composition, published in 1554. The prior of Santa Maria delle Grazie was pressing Leonardo to finish the *Last Supper*, and complained to Ludovico Sforza about the artist's slow work. Leonardo, 'almost laughing', explained to Ludovico:

Most excellent lord, there still remains to be done the head of Judas, that great traitor whom you know; for he deserves to be painted with a face fitting to such villainy. And although I could pick many from among those who accuse me, who would be wonderfully apt for Judas – nonetheless, so as not to embarrass them, for a year or more now I have taken myself to the Borghetto, where all the vile and ignoble people live, wicked and villainous for the most part, to see if I should come across a face that would be up to fulfilling an image of that wretch; nor have I been able to find it yet, but the moment it appears before me I will complete in a day all that remains to be done. Or if perhaps I don't find it, I will place there the face of the prior who is such a nuisance to me now, for he will be wonderfully suitable.[3]

This anecdote was adopted by Giorgio Vasari in his life of Leonardo published in 1568,[4] and from that much more widely read source it passed into common currency.

1. Clark and Pedretti 1968–9, I, p. 101.
2. *Loc. cit.* A small copy of the heads of Judas and Peter juxtaposed as in the mural (Milan, Biblioteca Ambrosiana, inv. F. 274 inf. 5) has repeatedly been claimed to be a copy of the next stage in Leonardo's sequence of preparatory studies for the *Last Supper*, but it appears to be no more than a copy of the finished composition.
3. Cinthio 1554, pp. 195f.; transcribed in Kwakkelstein 1994, p. 139.
4. Vasari 1965, p. 263.

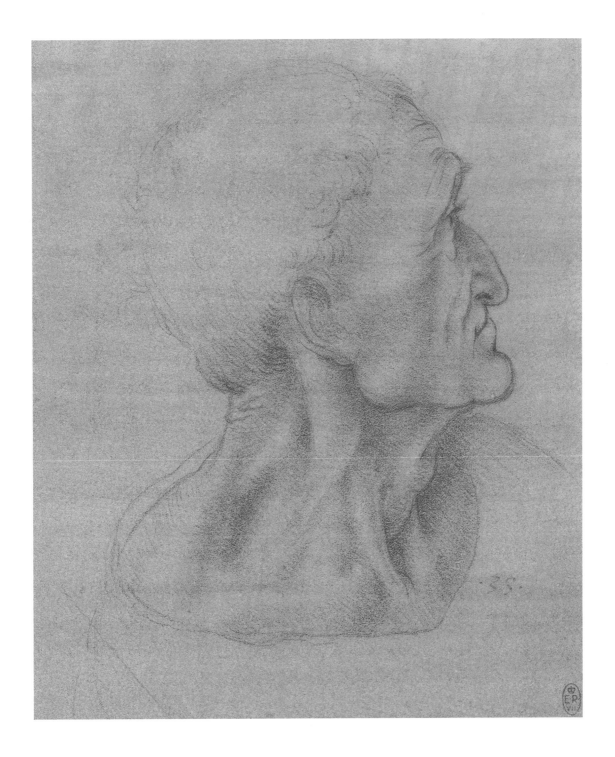

55

Attributed to CESARE DA SESTO (1477–1523), after Leonardo
The head of St Simon, after c.1495

Red chalk on red prepared paper
19.2 × 15.1 cm (7⁹⁄₁₆ × 5⁵⁄₁₆″)
Numbered by Melzi .21.
RL 12550

The head corresponds with that of the disciple at the far right of the *Last Supper*, probably St Simon (FIG. 45). Again the head gained a full beard in the painting; the unshaven chin and narrowed eyes of Leonardo's model make him appear more malevolent than Judas, and if Leonardo did indeed search for appropriate models for his composition one must wonder what his criteria were.

Though shaded from left to right in the manner of a left-handed artist, the drawing is a copy after a lost drawing by Leonardo and can be attributed to Cesare da Sesto, by comparison with a number of other drawings by Cesare in this red-on-red technique among the Melzi/Leoni sequence at Windsor.[1] There is another copy of the head (probably a copy of this drawing) at Windsor (FIG. 46), in red chalk on unprepared paper and consistent in style with other copies attributed to Francesco Melzi (CATS. 21, 38, 39). The presence of the Melzi copy and its probable model among the Windsor drawings might dispose of the theory that Melzi's drawings were 'replacement copies' made when he gave away the originals; this seems in any case unlikely, given his devoted custodianship of Leonardo's papers.[2]

1. The drawing was catalogued as 'Leonardo(?)' by Marani in Milan 2001, no. 37.
2. See Clark 1967.

FIG. 45 Detail of FIG. 40

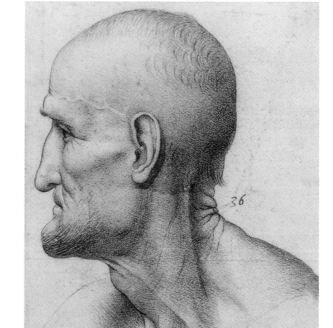

FIG. 46
Attributed to FRANCESCO MELZI (1491/3–c.1570), after Leonardo
The head of St Simon, c.1510–20
Red chalk, 18.5 × 14.8 cm (7⁵⁄₁₆ × 5¹³⁄₁₆″)
RL 12549

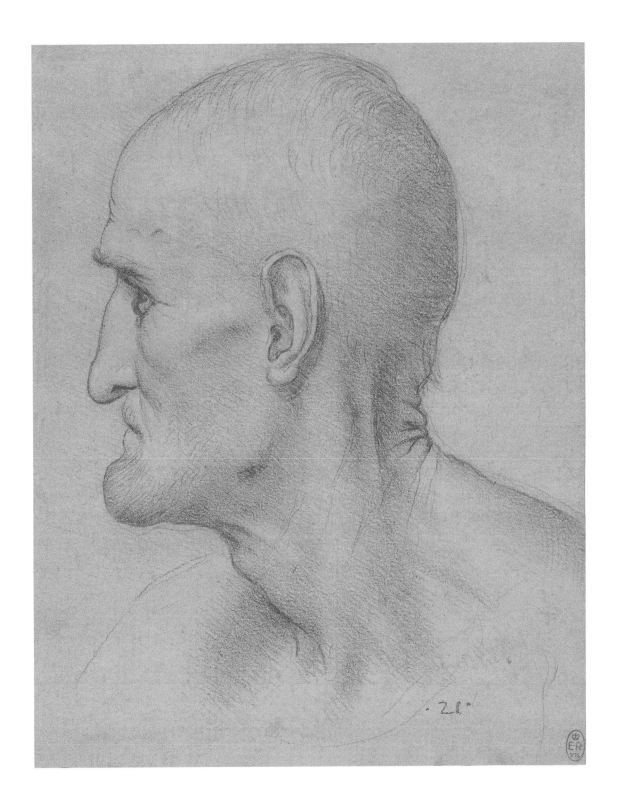

WOMEN

Leonardo had little interest in exploring a range of ideals of female beauty comparable to the male types that he developed (CATS. 15–25). Whether this should be related to the supposition that he was exclusively homosexual (though not necessarily actively so) throughout his life is a moot point.[1] While Leonardo's portraits of real women (see pp. 101–8) show confident, self-possessed individuals, his imaginary women conform much more closely to contemporary ideals of female behaviour. The position of women in Renaissance society was largely circumscribed by convention, but treatises of the period that touch on the conduct of women (from Leon Battista Alberti's *On the family* of *c*.1434 to Agnolo Firenzuola's *On the beauty of women*, completed in 1541) are less proscriptive than might be expected; they are generally concerned with humanist ideals of behaviour rather than with legal and social constraints. The most important virtue was chastity, but the ideal for female comportment, *modestia*, was not synonymous with submissiveness. The same standards of civilised conduct applied to both men and women: decorum and gravity, a reasonableness of manner, an avoidance of pomp and ostentation. The most notable difference in emphasis was the exhortation to women to observe stillness and sobriety of action, avoiding chatter and gossip and keeping the eyes modestly cast down.[2]

In his notes towards the *Treatise*, Leonardo accordingly stated that 'Women must be represented in modest attitudes, their legs close together, their arms closely folded, their heads lowered and somewhat on one side.'[3] The mature women in Leonardo's non-portrait paintings, and in the drawings presented here, do indeed all keep their eyes cast down, with their heads tipped at a graceful angle (with the exception of St Anne in FIG. 49, whose sideways glance at the Madonna has a narrative significance). The humility of the Madonna was a commonplace, and devotional texts routinely describe the grace and modesty of her actions; the downwards gaze of Leda, on the other hand, was a necessary corrective to the carnality of the subject of *Leda and the swan* – the modest nude was acceptably erotic, but a lascivious expression would

have rendered the painting obscene. The laugh of the *Benois Madonna* (St Petersburg, Hermitage State Museum) and the direct gaze of the Madonna in the *Annunciation* (Florence, Uffizi) were acceptable because Leonardo depicted them as girls, who had more freedom in their behaviour.

An incidental 'use' of women in the visual arts was as vehicles for fantastic attire. Leonardo viewed ostentation, particularly in the elderly, as worthy of mockery (CATS. 27, 39, 40), but throughout his life he had a love of personal adornment (CATS. 65–75). Many of his paintings of women, and all the drawings in this section, show elaborate headdresses or tightly braided and knotted coiffures that border on the fetishistic. This was not peculiar to Leonardo. The delights of hair were a theme of courtly love poetry, and depictions of ornate hairstyles were a common motif in the Florence of Leonardo's youth. He would have known studies by Andrea del Verrocchio of ideal female heads (FIG. 47), and indeed Giorgio Vasari noted, in his biography of Verrocchio, drawings of 'heads of women with lovely expressions and hairstyles, which because of their beauty Leonardo da Vinci was always imitating'.[4] Leonardo's list of his own drawings of the early 1480s included 'a head of a girl with tresses gathered in a knot' and 'a head with the hair dressed', as well as 'many drawings of knots' which reflect his fascination with elaborate patterning.[5]

Except in the eyes of certain ascetic theologians, adornment in itself carried no exclusive moral value, positive or negative (an issue distinct from the civic sumptuary laws of the period that attempted to limit conspicuous consumption and the flaunting of wealth). A tightly worked hairstyle could be a sign of vanity on Salome or of chastity on the Madonna; the hair worn loose and undressed was just as equivocal, and could be a sign either of unmarried, carefree youth or of immorality. The hair of the young Virgin of the *Annunciation* hangs loosely down over her shoulders, whereas both the *Madonna of the Carnation* (Munich, Alte Pinakothek) and the *Benois Madonna* have tight plaits running from the top of the head to intricate loops over the ears. Those paintings were

FIG. 47
ANDREA DEL VERROCCHIO (c.1435–88)
The head of a woman, c.1470–80
Black and white chalks, 31.8 × 26.5 cm (12½ × 10⁷⁄₁₆″)
London, British Museum, Department of Prints and
Drawings, inv. 1895-9-15-785

created primarily to have a devotional function, but
also to be beautiful in themselves; the *Leda*, on the
other hand, was painted solely as a beautiful image,
and the extreme contrivance of her dense coiffure was
a foil to the natural voluptuousness of her nude body.

1. On Leonardo and homosexuality see Pedretti 1991a;
    Marinoni 1992; and more generally, Saslow 1986.
2. See for instance Cropper 1976; Kelso 1978; Rogers 1988;
    Ajmar 2000; Knox 2000; Washington 2001–2, all with
    further bibliography.
3. Codex Ashburnham II, f. 17v; Richter 1939, no. 583.
4. Vasari 1965, p. 235.
5. Codex Atlanticus, f. 324r; Richter 1939, no. 680. On
    Leonardo's designs for knots and interlacing see
    Pedretti 1986, pp. 296–303.

56

LEONARDO DA VINCI
The head of St Anne, c.1510–15

Black chalk, wetted in places
18.8 × 13.0 cm (7⅜ × 5⅛″)
RL 12533

The subject of the *Madonna and Child with St Anne*
occupied Leonardo intermittently for the last two
decades of his life. He evolved three separate full-size
compositions, of which a cartoon (London, National
Gallery) and a painting (Paris, Musée du Louvre) survive in the original. The painting (FIG. 48) was probably worked on slowly from around 1508 onwards; it
was recorded by Antonio de Beatis in Leonardo's studio in France when he was visited by Cardinal Luigi of
Aragon on 10 October 1517, and remained unfinished in
the foreground landscape and the lower drapery of
St Anne. Twelve autograph studies of details for the
Louvre panel survive, and their apparent differences of
date suggest that they were executed as work on the
panel proceeded.[1] The present drawing is for the head
of St Anne, and in the absence of a full understanding
of the development of Leonardo's chalk style during
his later Milanese and Roman years, we can probably
do no better than to place it roughly between 1510
and 1515.

As an older woman St Anne was required to have a
covered head, and thus Leonardo could not indulge his
taste for decorative hairstyles. Instead he lavished his
attention on an elaborately folded and twisted headdress; as in the Leda studies (CATS. 58–61) the oblique
downwards gaze occupied Leonardo little, and the
headdress dwarfs both in scale and complexity the
rather small features of the saint. The head in the
painting is very different in character, for while the
form of the headdress was retained with no significant
change, the eyes, nose and mouth were rounded out,
regularised and enlarged.

Sigmund Freud made much of the apparent similarity of age of St Anne and the Madonna in the earlier
London cartoon of the *Madonna and Child with St Anne
and the infant Baptist* (FIG. 49), and the same observation could be applied to the Louvre painting. Freud's
essay *A Childhood Memory of Leonardo da Vinci*, first
published in 1910, was primarily an experiment in the
psychoanalysis of a historical figure, and attempted to

FIG. 48
LEONARDO DA VINCI and workshop, c.1510–19
The Madonna and Child with St Anne and a lamb
Oil on panel, 168 × 130 cm (66 × 51″)
Paris, Musée du Louvre

identify the impulses behind Leonardo's work in the supposed sexual experiences of his childhood. Freud's central proposal was that excessive love in Leonardo's childhood towards his natural mother, from whom he was separated as an infant, led to repression of his adult sexuality (for to love a woman would be a betrayal of his mother), and that this repression was sublimated into an urge to investigate. Freud further speculated that the experience of being taken from his natural mother and brought up in a household with a step-mother had given Leonardo, in effect, two mothers, and that the apparent similarity of age of the Madonna and St Anne in these late compositions was an expression of this deep feeling.[2] The truth may be simpler:

FIG. 49
LEONARDO DA VINCI
The Madonna and Child with St Anne and the infant Baptist, c.1508
Charcoal and black and white chalks
141.5 × 104.6 cm (55¾ × 41¼")
London, National Gallery

the heads look similar because they both approach Leonardo's late ideal of natural divinity, whether male or female – a slightly plump face and a gentle contented smile, celebrated in the *Mona Lisa* but just as insistent in both compositions of the *Madonna and St Anne*, in the *Leda* and in the Louvre *St John the Baptist*.[3]

1. Clayton 1996, pp. 132–6.
2. Freud 1910, and many later editions. See Collins 1997, pp. 56–61, for a balanced discussion of this aspect of Freud's theory, and *passim* for the battles that have been fought over the psychoanalysis of Leonardo.
3. Barolsky 1989.

57

LEONARDO DA VINCI (with additions)
The head of the Madonna
*c.*1510–15 and later

Red and black chalks, brush and dilute black ink,
white heightening, on pale red prepared paper
24.4 × 18.7 cm (9⅝ × 7⅜″)
RL 12534

Leonardo's hand is evident only in the intricate head-dress, for the face was worked up later by another artist. It cannot be discerned whether Leonardo had made any indications of the intended form of the face; even if he had not, it is telling that the later hand followed exactly the late Leonardesque type of large, heavy features and a downcast glance, the compelling invention that is found throughout Milanese art for the next couple of generations. The same process, or at least a significant strengthening of Leonardo's original drawing, might explain the discomforting aspects of a study in the Metropolitan Museum of Art, New York, for the head of the Virgin in the Louvre *St Anne* (FIG. 50), a drawing that also combines a beautiful and sophisticated study of the hair with rather rubbery modelling in the face.[1]

A headdress in this form does not occur in any work by Leonardo, but there is evidence of four late paintings of the *Madonna and Child* of which we have no trace, and the drawing could in principle have been a study for any one of these. The elaborate technique suggests a date after 1510, and thus it may have been drawn for a *Madonna and Child* mentioned by Vasari as having been painted for Baldassare Turini, an official to Pope Leo X, but this can be only a hypothesis.

1.   Bean 1982, no. 110; Trutty-Coohill 1993a, no. 18.

FIG. 50
LEONARDO DA VINCI (with additions?)
*The head of the Virgin, c.*1510–15
Black and coloured chalks, 20.3 × 15.6 cm (8 × 6⅛″)
New York, Metropolitan Museum of Art, inv. 51.90

58

LEONARDO DA VINCI
Studies for the head of Leda, c.1505–6

Pen and ink over black chalk
20.0 × 16.2 cm (7⅞ × 6⅜″), lower left corner cut
Numbered by Melzi *.11.*
RL 12516

Leda, the wife of Tyndareus, King of Sparta, was seduced by Jupiter in the form of a swan and bore two eggs, from which hatched Helen of Troy and Clytemnestra, and Castor and Pollux. Leonardo worked on two versions of a composition of *Leda and the swan*. The first, in which Leda kneels to embrace the swan, was probably under consideration by 1503, for Leonardo sketched the contorted figure three times on a sheet that also contains a study for the *Battle of Anghiari* (RL 12337). No patron is known, nor why Leonardo would otherwise have begun to work on this composition during one of the busiest periods of his life. Two further drawings show the kneeling pose fully developed,[1] but the extreme contrivance and instability of that format was abandoned in favour of a more elegant composition in which Leda stands. A carefully worked drawing in that form, if not a full-scale version, was completed by 1508 at the latest, for it was copied by Raphael (in a drawing also at Windsor) before he left Florence for Rome in that year.[2]

Over the next decade Leonardo executed a painting of the standing Leda, which was still in his possession at his death in France and passed to his assistant Salaì. The *Leda* was the most highly valued item in Salaì's estate after his death in 1524, and was soon sold back into France. The painting was seen by Cassiano dal Pozzo at Fontainebleau in 1625, but its deteriorating condition apparently led to its destruction some time between 1694 and 1775. Several painted copies of the composition are known, which agree in the form of the central group but differ in the backgrounds, suggesting that they were made from a cartoon in which the background was barely indicated, rather than from the finished panel.[3]

Four detailed studies of Leda's head survive (CATS. 58–61), all for the standing version.[4] It is striking how

little effort Leonardo seems to have expended on the face or expression of Leda; he quickly adopted his usual angled downward glance, and devoted all his energies to studying the most complicated of hairstyles. The style of these drawings points to a date of around 1505–6, when Leonardo's use of curvilinear modelling was fully developed. The watermark on CAT. 58 (an eagle in a circle) is Florentine and identical to that on one of the sheets of muscular standing nudes (RL 12630) associable with the later stages of the *Battle of Anghiari*; and another drawing by Raphael, preparatory for his Borghese *Christ carried to the tomb* of 1507, includes sketches of elaborate hairstyles that clearly betray knowledge of Leonardo's Leda head studies.[5]

The largest study in CAT. 58 is in the pose of the standing Leda, and the hairstyle appears to be in approximately the form on which Leonardo finally settled, for a closely similar arrangement is seen in most of the copies (FIG. 51). The two smaller studies below and to the left of the main drawing show the continuation of this coiffure at the back of Leda's head: the whorls around the temples with loose strands emerging from the centre are the same, and the subsidiary plaits hanging below the whorls are woven at the back into a dense criss-cross pattern. Of course it was unnecessary for Leonardo even to think about how Leda's hair might look from behind, and his care to do so can be attributed not to any practical considerations but only to his fascination and delight with the motif.

It was this version of Leda, with coils of hair at the side of the head, that seems to have been the model for the engraving of *A peasant embracing a beautiful woman* by Giovanni Antonio da Brescia[6] and, almost five centuries later, for Princess Leia (her name a modification of 'Leda') in George Lucas's film *Star Wars*, released in 1977.

FIG. 51
Copy after Leonardo
Leda and the swan, after 1515
Oil on panel, 96.5 × 74 cm (38 × 29″)
Wilton House, courtesy of the Earl of Pembroke and the
Trustees of the Wilton House Trust

1. Chatsworth, Devonshire Collection, Jaffé 1994, no. 880;
   Rotterdam, Museum Boymans-van Beuningen, Popham
   1946, no. 208.
2. Clayton 1999, no. 12.
3. For the project see most recently Vinci 2001.
4. A damaged drawing of the head of Leda in the Castello
   Sforzesco, executed in red chalk on red prepared paper, has

recently been championed as by Leonardo himself (Pedretti
1988a; Milan 1998–9b, p. 48). It seems, however, to be a copy
by one of Leonardo's more competent Milanese followers –
see Fiorio in Milan 1987–8, no. 44; Marani 1987, p. 48; Brown
1989, pp. 30–2.

5. Pouncey and Gere 1962, no. 11.
6. Hind 1948, V, p. 67, no. 16.

59

LEONARDO DA VINCI
*The head of Leda, c.*1505–6

Pen and ink over black chalk
17.7 × 14.7 cm (6¹⁵⁄₁₆ × 5¹³⁄₁₆″)
Numbered by Melzi *12*
RL 12518

The largest of Leonardo's head studies for the *Leda* retains the parallel plaits running over the top of the head seen in CAT. 58, but replaces the whorls at the temples by a pattern of interlacing. The hatching appears in many places (especially in the face) to have been done with the right hand, but it has the quality of Leonardo and the direction must be a consequence of the hatching system favoured by the artist at this time, in which the lines of shading were made to follow the implied form rather than simply lying on the surface of the paper.

60

LEONARDO DA VINCI
(with additions?)
The head of Leda, c.1505–6

Pen and ink
9.2 × 11.2 cm (3⅝ × 4⁷⁄₁₆″)
RL 12515

The hairstyle is essentially the same as in CAT. 58, and even more tightly bound. The drawing of the face is clumsy and may have been added later by a different hand, though it is perhaps no less attractive than the abandoned sketch to the lower left of CAT. 58. The idea that Leonardo was studying the hair alone, unconcerned with the effects of the face, is supported by the curious note, 'this kind [can be] taken off and put on without being damaged'. This implies that Leonardo conceived Leda's hair as a wig, and Françoise Viatte even suggested that the drawings might have had an ancillary function as studies for real wigs, perhaps for a theatrical production;[1] indeed it is hard to think how else to explain such a note.

1.   Viatte 1994, p. 53.

61

LEONARDO DA VINCI
(with additions?)
*The head of Leda, c.*1505–6

Pen and ink over black chalk
9.3 × 10.4 cm (3¹¹⁄₁₆ × 4⅛″)
RL 12517

Like CAT. 59, the drawing studies a densely interlaced
network of plaits over the ears, though without any
central plait running down the centre of the head. The
face is of poor quality and may well have been added
later by a pupil of Leonardo.

FANTASY AND COSTUME

The theme of this book has been Leonardo's investigation and transformation of the human (and animal) form, and he held that the greatest gift of the artist was the ability to conjure forms from the imagination. Most 'monstrosities', such as dragons and devils, had a fairly stable iconography, but if the artist wished to concoct a new beast, Renaissance theorists recommended a variant on (or the antithesis of) the method anciently attributed to the Greek painter Zeuxis, of creating the perfect human form by selecting the best and most beautiful parts from different models. Imaginary beasts were to be created by conjoining the parts of diverse real animals, and Leonardo himself recommended the practice in a note of *c.*1490–92:

> *How you should make an imaginary animal appear natural.*
> You know that you cannot invent animals without limbs each of which, in itself, must resemble those of some other animal. Hence if you wish to make an animal imagined by you appear natural, let us say a dragon, take for its head that of a mastiff or hound, with the eyes of a cat, the ears of a porcupine, the nose of a greyhound, the brow of a lion, the temples of an old cock, the neck of a terrapin.[1]

This passage is a literary exercise rather than the description of a specific invention, but while Leonardo seems never to have applied the Zeuxian method to the human body – his interest was in a single ideal rather than a composite beauty – he did follow this advice on the creation of monsters in CATS. 62 and 65, drawings executed some forty years apart.

Giorgio Vasari described Leonardo following this procedure on two occasions. When asked to paint a Medusa's head on a shield, Leonardo assembled:

> ... lizards, crickets, serpents, butterflies, locusts, bats, and various strange creatures of this nature; from all these he took and assembled different parts to create a fearsome and horrible monster ....
> Leonardo took so long over the work that the stench of the dead animals in his room became unbearable, although he himself failed to notice because of his great love of painting.[2]

And in three dimensions:

> To the back of a very odd-looking lizard ... he attached with a mixture of quicksilver some wings, made from the scales of other lizards, which quivered as it walked along. Then after he had given it eyes, horns, and a beard he tamed the creature, and keeping it in a box he used to show it to his friends and frighten the life out of them.[3]

Many comparable examples could be cited in the literature on art of the Renaissance, and need not be taken at face value in every case, though Vasari does state that the Medusa shield was bought by Ludovico Sforza, which might make a stronger case for the painting having actually existed. The point was to emphasise both the god-like creativity of the artist and to a certain degree (undoubtedly present in Vasari's two tales) the eccentricity of artistic genius.

The practice of assemblage had to be handled with care by the artist. CAT. 62 shows the discordant effect of simply drawing parts of different animals with little thought to their coherence; CATS. 63–5 are more successful, but attempting to anatomise their components only diminishes Leonardo's achievement in creating a novel and convincing beast. Understandably, most artists stuck to traditional formulae; despite never having seen one, we all know perfectly well what a devil or a dragon looks like, and for an artist to move too far away from these conventions in the pursuit of novelty would only risk incomprehension. Further, this form of *invenzione* could not really be applied to the human form. Grotesque distortion was acceptable, but an assemblage of diverse parts would achieve only a trivially ludicrous effect. Pure invention found its human application instead in costume and hair, as it always has done and always will do.

The Renaissance vogue for extravagant hairstyles has been discussed above (pp. 143–55), and the taste for extravagant clothing was just as important. Leonardo's love of beauty was not, like Michelangelo's, confined to his art, for he was finely turned out himself. The appendix to the brief biography by the Anonimo Gaddiano describes Leonardo's elegant hairstyle (CAT. 46) and adds that 'he wore a rose-coloured cloak which came only to his knees, although at the time long vestments were the custom.'[4] Leonardo also spent significant sums on clothes for his young companion Salaì: surviving memoranda mention a cloak of silvered cloth trimmed with green velvet that Leonardo had had made for the youth,[5] and three gold ducats that he gave him to buy a pair of rose-coloured hose.[6] Salaì's posthumous inventory lists strung stones, pearls, and suits of damask and velvet, suggesting that he profited well from Leonardo's luxurious tastes.[7]

Extravagance in clothing reached its most liberated form in the design of costumes for entertainments. Street processions were a prominent feature of Renaissance communal life; masques, dances and tournaments were staples of court entertainment; and though theatre had not yet reached its modern status, with fixed auditoria and professional troupes, plays were sporadically produced and scenes from Scripture were acted out in the streets at religious festivals. All these required costumes, from simple masks to full-length robes, and major artists often devoted much effort to devising settings and costumes for public and courtly events. The absence of any visual record of many of these great occasions is a serious lacuna in our understanding of the period.

Leonardo was employed as a salaried court artist for at least twenty-five years, or half his adult life: in Milan from the mid-1480s until 1499 under Ludovico Sforza, and then sporadically under the French from 1506 to 1511; for the Medici in Rome and Florence from 1513 to 1516; and at the court of Francis I in the Loire valley from 1516 until his death in 1519. His inventiveness and technical ingenuity would have been exploited for all manner of festivities during these periods, and the short but well-informed biography of Leonardo written by Paolo Giovio around 1527 recorded that 'his genius for invention was astounding, and he was the arbiter of all questions relating to beauty and elegance, especially pageantry.'[8]

A creative role for Leonardo has been suggested in many of the entertainments held at the courts at which he worked, though there is direct evidence for his participation in only a few. His first documented production was a staging of Bernardo Bellincioni's play *Paradiso*, one of the events held to celebrate the wedding of Gian Galeazzo Sforza – officially Duke of Milan, though in reality the vassal of his uncle Ludovico – to Isabella of Aragon, Princess of Naples, in January 1490. Leonardo's set-piece, known only through a description, was a representation of the cosmos, with the stars on the inside of a huge concave bowl, men dressed as the planets, and Paradise itself populated by singers. Six years later Leonardo produced a performance of Baldassare Taccone's *Danaë* in the house of Gianfrancesco Sanseverino, for which we have stage and costume designs (see CATS. 66–7). And some time around 1508, back in Milan, Leonardo staged a performance, probably of *Orfeo* by the Florentine poet and humanist Politian (Angelo Poliziano), for the French occupying governor of the city, Charles d'Amboise. We have drawings and notes of an ambitious recreation of the realm of Pluto in the form of a mountain:

> When Pluto's paradise is opened, then there may be devils placed in twelve pots like openings into hell. Here will be Death, the Furies, Cerberus, many naked children weeping; here are fires made of various colours that move by dancing …[9]

Our knowledge of Leonardo's participation in entertainments other than theatrical performances in the earlier part of his career is sparser still. In 1491 Ludovico Sforza finally consented to marriage to Beatrice d'Este, daughter of Ercole, the Duke of Ferrara; in the same month Ludovico's niece Anna was married to Alfonso d'Este, Beatrice's brother, and the celebrations of this double wedding outshone the nuptials of the legitimate Duke the previous year. The only reference to Leonardo's role is in a personal note about the misbehaviour of Salaì, and is almost accidental:

> On 26 January, I, being in the house of Messer Galeazzo da Sanseverino, was arranging the festival for his jousting, and certain footmen having undressed to try on some costumes of wild men for the said festival, Giacomo went to the purse of one of them which lay on the bed with other clothes and took out such money as was in it.[10]

Another passage describing the costume of a horse and rider does not mention the event directly, but we know from a contemporary description of the pageant that such a costume was executed:

Above the helmet place a half globe, which is to signify our hemisphere, in the form of a world; on which let there be a peacock, richly decorated, and with his tail spread over the group; and every ornament belonging to the horse should be of peacock's feathers on a gold ground .... The housing of the horse should be of plain cloth of gold closely sprinkled with peacock's eyes, and this holds good for all the housings of the horse and the man's dress; and the man's crest and his neck-chain are of peacock's feathers on a golden ground.[11]

Wild man costumes, as mentioned in the previous passage, were a common element of Renaissance pageantry, and a drawing of such a costume is found alongside sketches of ornate hats and tunics in Leonardo's Codex Forster III (f. 9v). That notebook is datable to around 1493, which would rule out a connection of the sketch with Galeazzo Sanseverino's joust, and suggests instead a link with the festivities surrounding the marriage, in March 1493, of Ludovico's other niece, Bianca Maria, to the Holy Roman Emperor, Maximilian. Though we have no written document of Leonardo's involvement with that event, it is likely that he played some organising role in most or all of the festivities held at the Sforza court in the 1490s. It must be emphasised, however, that ambitious stage designs and sumptuous costumes were not the sole preserve of Leonardo, and we should be cautious about crediting him with responsibility for every festivity held in a city in which he was resident.

In late 1516 Leonardo, aged 64, was invited to France to serve Francis I at the chain of royal palaces in the Loire valley. Like most young monarchs of the period Francis had a great taste for lavish entertainments, and we have detailed descriptions of several of the festivities held during 1518 (see CAT. 72). The multi-layered elegance of the costumes worn on these occasions is seen in Leonardo's contemporary designs, and it must be concluded that one of his roles at the French court was to provide fantastic designs for Francis's seamstresses. It is only from the very end of Leonardo's life that we have a significant number of detailed costume drawings in his hand (including CATS. 71–5), and they alone give some idea of the rich inventions that he must have devised on several occasions during his career.

1. Codex Ashburnham II, f. 29r; Richter 1939, no. 585. See Morel 1997, ch. 6.
2. Vasari 1965, p. 259.
3. *Ibid.*, p. 269.
4. Goldscheider 1959, p. 32.
5. Paris MS L, f. 94r; Richter 1939, no. 1523.
6. Codex Arundel, f. 229v; Richter 1939, no. 1525.
7. Marani in Venice 1992, p. 23; Shell and Sironi 1992, pp. 116 and 141–51.
8. Richter 1939, I, pp. 2–3.
9. Codex Arundel, f. 231v; Richter 1939, no. 678. See Pedretti 1964.
10. Paris MS C, f. 15v; Richter 1939, no. 1458. See Fumagalli 1960.
11. Codex Arundel, f. 250r; Richter 1939, no. 674. See Kemp 1981, p. 167; Pedretti 1984.

62

LEONARDO DA VINCI
*Sketches of dragons, c.*1478–80

Stylus, black chalk, pen and ink
15.9 × 24.3 cm (6¼ × 9⁹⁄₁₆″)
Numbered by Melzi *.52.*
RL 12370 (Pedretti 1987, no. 78)

Towards the end of his first Florentine period Leonardo worked on a composition of a mounted figure fighting a dragon (probably not intended to be a *St George*, as a contemporary sheet of studies in the Louvre, Paris, includes a variant in which two horsemen attack the dragon).[1] The motif finally evolved into a group of fighting horsemen in the background of the *Adoration of the Magi* of 1481. Here Leonardo studied four possibilities for the dragon: in the lower two and that at upper right it appears to reel away from the lance, though with the sheet turned anti-clockwise the last may be read as flying. The almost effaced sketch at upper left was drawn with the sheet inverted, and shows the dragon defeated, its head and wings slumped on the ground and its tail curled above like a plume of smoke from a dying fire.

The drawings conform to the usual advice to invent a monster by assembling the parts of different animals. The wings are half-bird, half-bat, the legs are a lion's, the head a dog's, the neck and tail like a snake; but the body resembles nothing so much as a plucked chicken, and Leonardo was remarkably uncertain in attaching the different parts to this torso – it is hard to distinguish front from back, and impossible to discern how the beast might look when not under attack.

1. Paris, Musée du Louvre, Rothschild Collection, inv. 7810; see Popham 1954.

63

Attributed to FRANCESCO MELZI
(1491/3–c.1570), after Leonardo
The head of a devil, after c.1510

Red, black and white chalks and a little grey wash
on red prepared paper, 21.8 × 15.0 cm (8⁹⁄₁₆ × 5⅞″)
Numbered by Melzi *42*

RL 12371

The drawing appears to be a faithful copy, most probably by Francesco Melzi, of a lost original by Leonardo.
Although human in structure, the devil has ram's
horns, ears like hairy wings, huge lips revealing peg
teeth, goitres like testicles hanging from its chin, pendulous breasts and bat's wings. Peter Meller noted that
these features resemble those of Barbariccia, the
leader of the demons in Canto 22 of Dante's *Inferno*, as
illustrated by Sandro Botticelli in his drawings to the
Divine Comedy.[1] As Dante does not describe Barbariccia,
it might be supposed that Leonardo knew and emulated Botticelli's drawing; but Leonardo's devil is perhaps just as close in detail to that in Albrecht Dürer's
woodcut of the *Angel with the key to the bottomless pit*
from the *Apocalypse* (1498). There was a tradition in the
depiction of devils as in all other motifs, and a similarity between Leonardo's devil and Botticelli's does not
prove that one was dependent upon the other.

On the reasonable assumption that the copy repli-
cates the size and technique of Leonardo's original,
the drawing was probably an independent work, an
exemplar of *invenzione*, perhaps to be given to a friend
or patron. In this it parallels Leonardo's elaborate sheets
of the 1490s, such as CAT. 41, but the combination of
media seen here, three types of chalk with wash on
prepared paper, is found only (so far as we know) in
Leonardo's drawings of the period 1508–15 or there-
abouts. It therefore has more in common with the
finished heads of the last decade of Leonardo's life
(CATS. 17–25) than with the Sforza-period narratives and
allegories. Melzi had joined Leonardo's studio in Milan
by 1510; the watermark on the sheet (an eight-petalled
flower) is Milanese, and this copy may thus have been
made by the youth immediately before the original
was given to its intended recipient.

1. London 2000, pp. 96f. Meller (1955) also claimed that several
   of Leonardo's other drawings (including CATS. 65 and 72–4)
   were studies to Dante. Of these, the most convincing is the
   Pointing woman in a landscape (RL 12581), which Meller
   claimed to be Matelda appearing to Dante, Virgil and
   Statius in Canto XXVIII of *Purgatorio*. But the seemingly
   random selection of passages from the *Divine Comedy* that
   Meller thought were illustrated, and the diversity of date,
   technique and scale of the drawings that he assembled,
   must militate against his theory as a whole.

64

LEONARDO DA VINCI

Two heads of grotesque animals, c.1490–95

Pen and ink over black chalk
13.8 × 17.4 cm (5⁷⁄₁₆ × 6⁷⁄₈″)
Numbered by Melzi 40.
RL 12367 (Pedretti 1987, no. 154)

The head on the right is clearly canine, a long-haired hound with a grotesquely long lower lip that was an accepted sign of inanity (as in the 'foolish hanging of thy nether lip,' in Falstaff's mockery of Prince Hal).[1] The other head is less easy to characterise: it has a mouth like a pug dog, a lion's mane, ears like a shaggy bear, and strange wrinkled flaps from the brow hanging down the cheeks. The bit and bridle that emerge from its mouth would suggest that this was a study for a fantastic mask to be worn by a costumed servant pulling a chariot or float in some procession. Almost the same head is seen in profile in another drawing at Windsor (FIG. 52), reinforcing the impression that the head was intended to be realised in three dimensions. There are no similar clues to the function of the head on the right, which may have been no more than a caprice.

The strange form of the left-hand animal's brow may be explained by turning the drawing upside down (FIG. 53). The wrinkles between the eyes now become a nose, the ears become an unkempt beard, and the flaps over the cheeks become fantastic ears: a new face is created, in too contrived a manner to be mere accident. Such pictorial tricks were famously produced by Giuseppe Arcimboldo at the Habsburg court in the later sixteenth century, and it is conceivable that inventions in this manner by Leonardo were known to Arcimboldo before he left Milan in 1562. It is hard to see how the trick might have been effected in a full-head mask, but Leonardo's constant exploration of the possible was not always anchored in practicalities.

The style of the drawing, with smooth parallel hatching, dates it to the first half of the 1490s. Giuseppina Fumagalli sought to connect the drawing with Galeazzo Sanseverino's festivities of 1491, for which we know Leonardo designed costumes of wild men, but this can only be a hypothesis.[2]

Sketched in black chalk on the verso, and cut by the trimming of the recto, is a grotesque head in right profile with huge ears (FIG. 54), unrelated to any other work by Leonardo. It is rubbed and thus difficult to judge, but there seems no compelling reason to deny Leonardo's authorship.

1. William Shakespeare, *Henry IV Part I*, Act 2, Scene 4.
2. Fumagalli 1960, pp. 153–6.

FIG. 52 *(above)*
LEONARDO DA VINCI
The head of a grotesque animal, c.1490–95
Pen and ink, 11.1 × 6.9 cm (4⅜ × 2¹¹⁄₁₆″)
RL 12368

FIG. 53 *(right)* Detail of CAT. 64, inverted

FIG. 54 *(far right)* Detail of verso of CAT. 64

40.

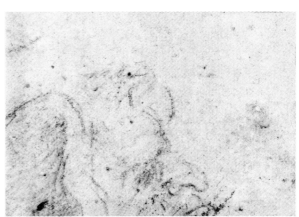

65

LEONARDO DA VINCI

A design for a costume of an imaginary beast, c.1517–18

Pen and ink over black chalk
18.8 × 27.0 cm (7⅜ × 10⅝″), upper left corner cut
Numbered by Melzi *.29*.
RL 12369 (Pedretti 1987, no. 156)

This is probably a design for an entertainment held during Leonardo's last years at the French court (see CATS. 71–5). The proportions and the manner in which the body and legs are articulated suggest that it was to house two men, in the manner of a pantomime horse. A clawed arm sketched in black chalk can be seen emerging from the side of the head, at the natural height of a man whose legs formed the front legs of the beast and who was supporting the oversized head on his shoulders. In this respect the creature is very similar to traditional Chinese festival dragons, but it would be inaccurate to call the present beast a dragon. Italian dragons of the period were winged and reptilian, as seen in CAT. 62; this has more of the character of a terrible horned dog with a serpentine tail. It is reminiscent of Leonardo's suggestion of *c.*1492 on composing a dragon, beginning with '[the head] of a mastiff or hound' (p. 157), but there is no reason to suppose that this is in any sense an illustration of his note of twenty-five years earlier.[1]

1. Meller (1955, p. 151) related the drawing to the description of the six-legged monster who consumes the burglar Cianfa dei Donati in Canto xxv of Dante's *Inferno*. Other than the presence of six 'legs' and a tail there is nothing to support this; see CAT. 63.

66

LEONARDO DA VINCI

A mask in the form of a human face, c.1496

Pen and ink
6.7 × 6.8 cm (2⅝ × 2¹¹⁄₁₆″), irregular
Numbered by Melzi *26*.
RL 12589

The mask has no specific character: it disguises rather than creates an identity. Like CATS. 31–6, this and the following three fragments were cut (probably by Francesco Melzi) from larger sheets of studies by Leonardo. The parent sheet of the present sketch (Codex Atlanticus f. 318b) consists mainly of mechanical and geometrical studies identical in character to those on a companion sheet (f. 318a) bearing the date 2 January 1496. It is thus likely that the mask is a costume study for a performance of Baldassare Taccone's play *Danaë*, held in the house of Gianfrancesco Sanseverino in Milan on 31 January 1496, for which

Leonardo seems to have designed the stage set and costumes. The cast list in Leonardo's hand has survived, together with a sketch for the stage set, in the Metropolitan Museum of Art, New York (FIG. 55), showing the figure of Jupiter in a flaming mandorla flanked by niches.[1]

1. Bean 1982, no. 108; Trutty-Coohill 1993a, no. 9. On a sheet in the Codex Atlanticus (f. 358v-b, the parent sheet of CAT. 67, also datable to January 1496) is another stage in steep perspective, though the set does not resemble that on the New York sheet.

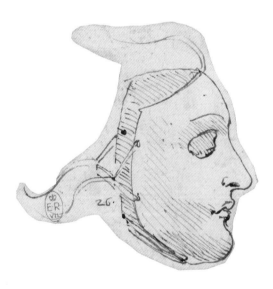

67

LEONARDO DA VINCI

The head of a man in right profile,
*wearing a plumed headdress, c.*1496

Pen and ink
6.3 × 4.2 cm (2½ × 1⅝″), irregular
Numbered by Melzi 19.
RL 12461

The headdress is quite simple, a band with wings from
the temples and plumes at the back. The drawing was
cut from Codex Atlanticus f. 358v-b, a sheet mainly of
mechanical drawings for a needle-making machine
studied again on Codex Atlanticus f. 318r-a, dated 2
January 1496. It is thus likely that this sketch was, like
CAT. 66, a costume for Taccone's *Danaë*. Kate Steinitz
proposed that the head might be that of King Acrisius,
the father of Danaë,[1] but the winged headdress suggests instead that he is a rather aged Mercury, whose
part was to be played (according to Leonardo's cast list,
FIG. 55) by one Gianbattista da Osimo.

1. Steinitz 1964.

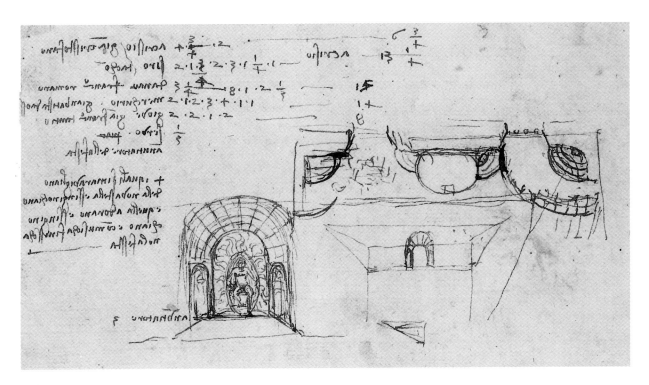

FIG. 55
LEONARDO DA VINCI
A stage design and cast list (detail), *c.*1496
Pen and ink, 20.2 × 13.3 cm (7¹⁵⁄₁₆ × 5¼″) overall
New York, Metropolitan Museum of Art, inv. 17.142.2

68

LEONARDO DA VINCI
*A study of a winged helmet with a
face-shaped visor, c.1485–90*

Pen and ink
4.0 × 4.6 cm (1⁹⁄₁₆ × 1¹³⁄₁₆″), irregular
RL 12588

69

LEONARDO DA VINCI
*Two studies of a helmet with a
face-shaped visor, c.1485–90*

Pen and ink
6.0 × 10.2 cm (2⅜ × 4″), lower left corner cut
Numbered by Melzi 49.
RL 12590

The fragments are clearly related, and though no parent sheet has been identified the rough style of the penwork indicates a date in the later 1480s, probably not long after Leonardo entered the service of Ludovico Sforza. The drawings show metal parade helmets with hinged visors, rather than ephemeral costumes in papier mâché, stiffened textile or leather. Helmets with hinged visors in the form of a human face had been known since antiquity,[1] and would have been familiar to the sophisticated Milanese armourers of Leonardo's day. It is thus possible that Leonardo was simply jotting down variants on a form that he had seen in use, rather than working on a design.

1. See for example New York 1998–9, nos 6 and 15. For armourers in Milan in Leonardo's time, and the influence of the antique on contemporary armour, *ibid.*, pp. 1–18.

70

LEONARDO DA VINCI

A design for a musical elephant costume,
c.1508–10

Black chalk
19.7 × 28.0 cm (7¾ × 11″), cut and repaired
RL 12585 (Keele and Pedretti 1979, no. 120)

The drawing is a study for the costume of a mounted masquerader, with an elephant's head, ragged ears, a curving trumpet on top of the head, long narrow wings hanging down from the shoulders, a pot belly and a curly tail. A wind instrument is integrated into the trunk, and Emanuel Winternitz suggested that the whole costume was a bagpipe, with the bag contained in the belly and the drone over the head.[1] The wonderful conceit of an equestrian elephant playing a tune on its own trunk shows why Leonardo was in such demand as a festival designer.

The roughness of the chalk, especially in the horse, suggests that Leonardo left the drawing unfinished, and it is not easy to date it on style alone. Studies for a cloistered courtyard on the verso of the sheet, showing through to the recto, may be connected with Leonardo's project for a residence for Charles d'Amboise, the governor of Milan during Leonardo's second period in the city, and the costume study may thus have been made for some festival organised by the French in Milan around 1508–10.

1. Winternitz 1974, p. 129.

71

LEONARDO DA VINCI

A design for a helmet, and other studies,
c.1517–18

Pen and ink over black chalk on rough paper
25.1 × 14.5 cm (9⅞ × 5¹¹⁄₁₆")
Numbered by Melzi .44.
RL 12329 (Pedretti 1987, no. 159)

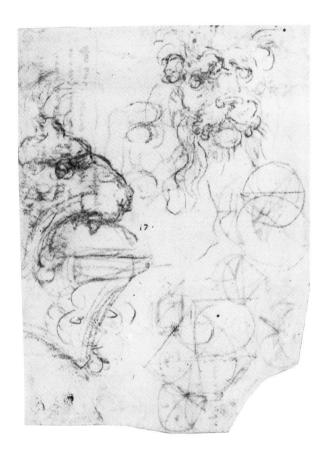

The drawing is surprisingly crude for Leonardo, and
the layout of the page is not as attractive as usual, but
there is no reason to doubt his authorship of the helmet and the horse. Weaker drawings done with the
paper the other way up, of the head of a woman,
mountain peaks and a grotesque bust with outstretched arm may be the work of an assistant. In part
the coarseness is a result of the rough surface of the
paper, which has been insufficiently sized, so that in
places the ink has bled. Paper of this type, with an orb
watermark, was used by Leonardo during his last years
in France,[1] a dating that is consistent with the style of
the present sketches.

The helmet is surmounted by a lion's head with a
short dense mane and what seems to be a plumed
horn. Lions' heads were a standard motif of decorated
armour – a roaring head is seen on Leonardo's early
Bust of a warrior (FIG. 9, p. 51), and ten years before the
present study he had drawn a very similar head atop a
helmet (FIG. 56).[2] CAT. 71 may have been a study for
jousting armour for the French court, but there are
few firm links between Leonardo's drawings and
actual projects in his last years.

1. Clayton 1996, pp. 140–41.
2. See New York 1998–9, no. 8, for a late fifteenth-century
    Italian helmet in the form of a lion's head.

FIG. 56
LEONARDO DA VINCI
A lion's head, a helmet surmounted by a lion's head,
and geometrical studies, c.1508
Black chalk, 15.2 × 11.3 cm (6 × 4⁷⁄₁₆")
RL 12586

72

LEONARDO DA VINCI
A masquerader as an exotic pikeman,
c.1517–18

Black chalk, pen and ink, wash, on rough paper
27.3 × 18.3 cm (10¾ × 7³⁄₁₆″)
Numbered by Melzi *86*
RL 12575

CATS. 65 and 71–5 can be dated to Leonardo's last years in France, in the service of the young Francis I.[1] This was a period of extravagant festivals at the French court; detailed descriptions survive, by the Mantuan secretary Stazio Gadio, of the entertainments held in January 1518 in honour of the young Federico Gonzaga of Mantua, then completing his education at the French court, and in May of the same year to celebrate both the baptism of the Dauphin and the wedding of the king's niece Madeleine de la Tour d'Auvergne to Lorenzo di Piero de' Medici, Leonardo's patron three years earlier in Florence.[2]

While the costumes described by Gadio do not correspond exactly with Leonardo's drawings, they are close enough in general effect and in many details to suggest that the drawings are studies for costumes to be worn at these or similar events. For instance Federico Gonzaga was described at one event as:

> very showy, dressed as a lansquenet, with half-boots, one completely dark, the other less dark, edged with a white and yellow riband cut in the German manner, a tunic half of satin, the edge of silver cloth, and golden cloth made into scales, with a German-style shirt worked with gold, and over this a cape of dark cloth fitted with a riband of gold and silver cloth made in the French manner …

This richness and layering of textiles is exactly what Leonardo was aiming at in CATS. 72-5. The use of parti-coloured material was decorative but also carried a loaded meaning – striped, checked and scalloped clothing was associated with the German and Swiss mercenary soldiers then employed throughout Europe, and with fools, minstrels and prostitutes. The dignified guests of Francis I were thus dressing up not just exotically, but in something equivocal and even a little risqué.[3]

---

1. For the dating see Clayton 1996, pp. 140–41, 150–54.
2. For Gadio's descriptions see Solmi 1924, pp. 347–56, and Shearman 1978.
3. Mellinkoff 1993, pp. 3–32, for the significance of patterned clothing.

73

LEONARDO DA VINCI
A masquerader on horseback, c.1517–18

Pen and ink over black chalk on rough paper
24.0 × 15.2 cm (9⁷⁄₁₆ × 6″)
Numbered by Melzi .87.
RL 12574

CAT. 73 is on the same porridgy paper as CAT. 72, and as the rider also carries a spear and has a sword by his side, he may well have been drawn as a study for the same entertainment. The hat is ultimately based on that worn by the Byzantine Emperor John VIII Palaeologus at the Council of Ferrara in 1438, as immortalised in the celebrated portrait medallion by Pisanello (FIG. 57); this type of hat subsequently became a signifier of eastern exoticism in paintings of the journey of the Magi and so on. The ribbons, plumes, fringes, quilted sleeves and breeches, and spotted furs of the costume would have created an effect of startling richness.

74

LEONARDO DA VINCI
A standing masquerader, c.1517–18

Black chalk
21.4 × 10.7 cm (8⁷⁄₁₆ × 4³⁄₁₆″)
Numbered by Melzi 85
RL 12577

The figure appears rather androgynous, but the stance with legs planted apart probably rules out the possibility that it is a woman. He seems to hold the edge of a long skirt up to the waist, to show the scalloped edges of the tunic and a sheer underskirt that reveals the left leg to the top of the thigh. This may have been Leonardo's way of indicating the structure of the costume to the seamstresses, though a companion drawing (FIG. 58), of a costume with an even more ornate tunic, shows a full sheer skirt that displays the whole of both legs.

The paper of CATS. 74 and 75 and FIG. 58 is much finer than that of CATS. 72 and 73, but both sheets bear a French watermark (a small fleur de lys in a shield, surmounted by a cross with three nails) that again dates the drawings to the last years of Leonardo's life. The highly atmospheric handling of black chalk is typical of his latest drawings.

FIG. 57 *(left)*
PISANELLO (1395–1455)
Portrait medal of the Emperor John VIII Palaeologus, 1438
Bronze, diameter 10.3 cm (4¹⁄₁₆″)
London, British Museum, Department of Coins and Medals, inv. George III Naples 9

FIG. 58 *(opposite, overleaf)*
LEONARDO DA VINCI
A standing masquerader, c.1517–18
Black chalk, 21.5 × 11.2 cm (8⁷⁄₁₆ × 4⁷⁄₁₆″)
RL 12576

74

FIG. 58

75

LEONARDO DA VINCI
The bust of a masquerader in right profile,
c.1517–18

Black chalk, rubbed with red chalk
17.0 × 14.6 cm (6¹¹⁄₁₆ × 5¾″)
Numbered by Melzi *.39.*
RL 12508

Though the features and hairstyle appear to be the same as in FIG. 58, the figure here has a high-waisted dress and pronounced bust, and must be female. The convergence of both male and female to a single type, with smooth, fleshy features, is a marked aspect of Leonardo's late work (see CAT. 56). The drawing is presumably a costume study for the same event as FIG. 58 and CAT. 74, though the profile format gives it the air of an independent ideal head. The red chalk is very indistinct but coincides too closely with the forms of the figure to be accidental offsetting, and must have been lightly rubbed on by Leonardo to give a colouristic effect unusual in his late drawings.

Clark thought the head was 'derived from an antique, either a coin or a gem', without citing comparable examples.[1] The hair is wound around the head and knotted, with a tail emerging from the knot, and groomed at the front into a shell-like crest; in concept this is closer to the ideal heads of Michelangelo and the Florentine Mannerists, and of the Fontainebleau School, than to Leonardo's earlier drawings such as the 'wig' worn by Leda (CATS. 58–61). Direct borrowings are hard to pin down, and the tradition of fantastic heads was not sustained by Leonardo alone in the early sixteenth century, but artists active in both Florence and Fontainebleau could have known Leonardo's late designs. Andrea del Sarto spent a short spell at the French court in 1518–19 before returning to Florence, and would surely have met Leonardo; Rosso Fiorentino arrived in France in 1530 and Primaticcio two years later. While the drawings discussed in this book had by then returned to Italy with Melzi, other designs by Leonardo – and maybe some actual costumes – were probably still in circulation at the French court.

1. Clark and Pedretti 1968–9, I, p. 89.

BIBLIOGRAPHY

AGOSTI 1990
G. Agosti, *Bambaia e il classicismo lombardo*, Turin 1990

AJMAR 2000
M. Ajmar, 'Exemplary women in Renaissance Italy: ambivalent models of behaviour?', in *Women in Italian Renaissance Culture and Society*, ed. L. Panizza, Oxford 2000, pp. 244–64

ALBERICI 1992
C. Alberici, 'Leonardo e l'incisione: qualche aggiunta', *Raccolta Vinciana*, XXIV, 1992, pp. 9–53

ALBERTI 1972
L.B. Alberti, *On Painting and On Sculpture*, ed. and trans. C. Grayson, London 1972

ANGIOLILLO 1979
M. Angiolillo, *Leonardo. Feste e teatri*, Naples 1979

ARLATI 1989
A. Arlati, 'Gli Zingari nello stato di Milano', *Lacio Drom*, XXV(2), 1989, pp. 4–11

ARONBERG LAVIN 1981
M. Aronberg Lavin, 'The Joy of the Bridegroom's Friend: Smiling Faces in Fra Filippo, Raphael and Leonardo', in *Art, the Ape of Nature. Studies in Honor of Horst W. Janson*, New York 1981, pp. 193–210

BAMBACH CAPPEL 1994
C. Bambach Cappel, 'On *La testa proporzionalmente degradata* – Luca Signorelli, Leonardo, and Piero della Francesca's *De prospectiva pingendi*', in *Florentine Drawing at the Time of Lorenzo the Magnificent*, ed. E. Cropper, Bologna 1994, pp. 17–43

BAROLSKY 1989
P. Barolsky, 'The Mysterious Meaning of Leonardo's St John the Baptist', *Source*, III, 1989, pp. 12–15

BAROLSKY 1992
P. Barolsky, 'La Gallerani's *Galée*', *Source*, XII, 1992, pp. 13–14

BARRYTE 1990
B. Barryte, 'The Ill-Matched Couple', *Achademia Leonardi Vinci*, III, 1990, pp. 133–9

BEAN 1982
J. Bean, *15th and 16th Century Italian Drawings in the Metropolitan Museum of Art*, New York 1982

BELLONI 1954
L. Belloni, 'Per il toracoparassita di Leonardo', *Rendiconti dell'Istituto Lombardo di Scienza e Lettere*, LXXXVII, 1954, pp. 157–66

BELLONI 1982
L. Belloni, 'Elementi anatomici, morbosi e abnormi nei disegni di Leonardo', in *Leonardo e l'età di ragione*, ed. E. Belloni and P. Rossi, Milan 1982, pp. 455–63

BELTRAMI 1919
L. Beltrami, 'Il volto di Leonardo', *Per il IV centenario della morte di Leonardo da Vinci*, Bergamo 1919, pp. 75ff.

BERRA 1993
G. Berra, 'La storia dei canoni proporzionali del corpo umano e gli sviluppi in area lombarda alla fine del Cinquecento', *Raccolta Vinciana*, XXV, 1993, pp. 159–310

BIALOSTOCKI 1955
J. Bialostocki, 'New Observations on Joos van Cleve', *Oud-Holland*, LXX, 1955, pp. 121–9

BIALOSTOCKI 1959
J. Bialostocki, '"Opus quinque dierum": Dürer's "Christ among the Doctors" and its Sources', *Journal of the Warburg and Courtauld Institutes*, XXII, 1959, pp. 17–34

BODMER 1931
H. Bodmer, *Leonardo. Des Meisters Gemälde und Zeichnungen*, London 1931

BONTEMPELLI 1922
M. Bontempelli, ed., *Il Poliziano, Il Magnifico, Lirici del Quattrocento*, Florence 1922

BORA 1989
G. Bora, 'Da Leonardo all'Accademia della Val di Bregno', *Raccolta Vinciana*, XXIII, 1989, pp. 73–101

BORRMANN 1994
N. Borrmann, *Kunst und Physiognomik. Menschendeutung und Menschendarstellung im Abendland*, Cologne 1994

BRAUNFELS-ESCHE 1994
S. Braunfels-Esche, 'Aspekte der Bewegung, Umrisse von Leonardos Proportions- und Bewegungslehre', in *Festschrift Lorenz Dittmann*, Frankfurt am Main 1994, pp. 57–72

BRIDGEMAN 1998
J. Bridgeman, '"Condecenti et netti ...": Beauty, dress and gender in Italian Renaissance art', in *Concepts of Beauty in Renaissance Art*, ed. F. Ames-Lewis and M. Rogers, Aldershot 1998, pp. 44–51

BROWN 1983
D.A. Brown, 'Leonardo and the Idealised Portrait in Milan', *Arte Lombarda*, LXVII, 1983, pp. 102–16

BROWN 1989
D.A. Brown, review of Milan 1987–8, *Raccolta Vinciana*, XXIII, 1989, pp. 27–32

BROWN 1990
D.A. Brown, 'Leonardo and the Ladies with the Ermine and the Book', *Artibus et Historiae*, XXII, 1990, pp. 47–61

BROWN 1994
D.A. Brown, 'Leonardo's "Head of an old man" in Turin: portrait or self-portrait?', in *Studi di storia dell'arte in onore di Mina Gregori*, Milan 1994, pp. 75–8

BROWN 1998
D.A. Brown, *Leonardo da Vinci. Origins of a Genius*, New Haven and London 1998

CAMPBELL 1990
L. Campbell, *Renaissance Portraits*, New Haven and London 1990

CAROLI 1984
F. Caroli, *L'arte dalla psicologia alla psicoanalisi. Teoria artistica e ricerche sul profondo dal XV al XX secolo*, Bologna 1984

CAROLI 1991
F. Caroli, *Leonardo. Studi di fisiognomica*, Milan 1991

CAROLI 1995a
F. Caroli, *Storia della fisiognomica. Arte e psicologia da Leonardo a Freud*, Milan 1995

CAROLI 1995b
F. Caroli, 'Fisiognomica come nuovo Umanesimo: da Leonardo a Freud', *Achademia Leonardi Vinci*, VIII, 1995, pp. 167–70

CASTELFRANCHI VEGAS 1983
L. Castelfranchi Vegas, '"Retracto del naturale": considerazioni sulla ritrattistica lombarda degli anni fra Quattrocento e Cinquecento', *Paragone*, XXXIV (401–3), 1983, pp. 64–71

CATTABIANI 1996
A. Cattabiani, *Florario. Miti, leggende e simboli di fiori e piante*, Milan 1996

CHASTEL 1978
A. Chastel, 'Les capitaines antiques affrontés dans l'art florentin du XVe siècle', in *Fables, Formes, Figures*, I, Paris 1978, pp. 237–46

CIAPPONI 1984
L.A. Ciapponi, 'Fra Giocondo da Verona and his Edition of Vitruvius', *Journal of the Warburg and Courtauld Institutes*, XLVII, 1984, pp. 72–86

CINTHIO 1554
G.G. Cinthio, *Discorsi intorno al comporre dei Romanzi, delle Comedie, e delle Tragedie, e di altre maniere di poesie*, Venice 1554

CLARK 1935
K. Clark, *A Catalogue of the Drawings of Leonardo da Vinci in the Collection of His Majesty The King at Windsor Castle*, 2 vols, Cambridge 1935

CLARK 1967
K. Clark, 'Francesco Melzi as Preserver of Leonardo da Vinci's Drawings', in *Studies in Renaissance and Baroque Art Presented to Anthony Blunt on his 60th Birthday*, London 1967, pp. 24–5

CLARK 1969
K. Clark, 'Leonardo and the Antique', in *Leonardo's Legacy*, ed. C.D. O'Malley, Berkeley and Los Angeles 1969, pp. 1–34

CLARK AND PEDRETTI 1968–9
K. Clark and C. Pedretti, *The Drawings of Leonardo da Vinci in the Collection of Her Majesty The Queen at Windsor Castle*, 3 vols, London 1968–9

CLAYTON 1996
M. Clayton, *Leonardo da Vinci. A Curious Vision*, London 1996

CLAYTON 1999
M. Clayton, *Raphael and his Circle. Drawings from Windsor Castle*, London 1999

CLAYTON 2002
M. Clayton, 'Leonardo's *Gypsies*, and the *Wolf with the Eagle*', *Apollo*, August 2002

COGLIATI ARANO 1992
L. Cogliati Arano, *Leonardo e la rappresentazione della terza età* (XXXI Lettura Vinciana), Florence 1992

COLENBRANDER 1992
H. Colenbrander, 'Hands in Leonardo Portraiture', *Achademia Leonardi Vinci*, V, 1992, pp. 37–43

COLLINS 1997
B. Collins, *Leonardo, Psychoanalysis and Art History*, Evanston IL 1997

COUPE 1967
W.A. Coupe, 'Ungleiche Liebe – a Sixteenth-Century Topos', *Modern Language Review*, LXII, 1967, pp. 661–71

CROPPER 1976
E. Cropper, 'On beautiful women, Parmigianino, Petrarchismo and the vernacular style', *Art Bulletin*, LVIII, 1976, pp. 374–94

CROPPER 1985
E. Cropper, 'The Beauty of Women: Problems in the Rhetoric of Renaissance Portraiture', in *Rewriting the Renaissance*, ed. M.W. Ferguson *et al.*, Chicago 1985, pp. 175–90

CROPPER 1995
E. Cropper, 'The Place of Beauty in the High Renaissance and its Displacement in the History of Art', in *Place and Displacement in the Renaissance*, ed. A. Vos, Binghampton NY 1995, pp. 159–205

CUNNALLY 1988
J. Cunnally, 'Leonardo and the Horses of Nero', *Burlington Magazine*, CXXX, 1988, pp. 689–90

CUNNALLY 1993
J. Cunnally, 'Numismatic Sources for Leonardo's Equestrian Monuments', *Achademia Leonardi Vinci*, VI, 1993, pp. 67–78

CUZIN 1977
J.-P. Cuzin, *La diseuse de bonne aventure de Caravage*, Paris 1977

DILLON 1994
G. Dillon, 'Una serie di figure grottesche', in *Florentine Drawing at the Time of Lorenzo the Magnificent*, ed. E. Cropper, Bologna 1994, pp. 217–30

ECO 1986
U. Eco, *Art and Beauty in the Middle Ages*, New Haven and London 1986

ERASMUS 1979
D. Erasmus, *The Praise of Folly*, trans. C. Miller, New Haven and London 1979

EVANS 1969
E. Evans, 'Physiognomy in the Ancient World', *Transactions of the American Philosophical Society*, LIX, 1969, pp. 3–101

FABRIZIO-COSTA 1997
S. Fabrizio-Costa, '"Elena quando si specchiava …"', *Achademia Leonardi Vinci*, X, 1997, pp. 89–100

FAVARO 1917
A. Favaro, 'Il canone di Leonardo sulle proporzioni del corpo umano', *Atti del Reale Istituto Veneto di Scienze, Lettere ed Arti*, LXXVII, 1917, pp. 167–227

FAVARO 1918
A. Favaro, 'Misure e proporzioni del corpo umano secondo Leonardo', *Atti del Reale Istituto Veneto di Scienze, Lettere ed Arti*, LXXVIII, 1918, pp. 110–90

FIORIO 1982
M.T. Fiorio, *Leonardeschi in Lombardia*, Milan 1982

FIORIO 2000
M.T. Fiorio, *Giovanni Antonio Boltraffio*, Milan 2000

FIRENZUOLA 1992
A. Firenzuola, *On the Beauty of Women*, ed. and trans. K. Eisenbichler and J. Murray, Philadelphia 1992

FLORENCE 1992
Il disegno fiorentino del tempo di Lorenzo il Magnifico, exh. cat., ed. A. Petrioli Tofani, Florence, Uffizi, 1992

FREUD 1910
S. Freud, *Ein Kinderheitserinnerung des Leonardo da Vinci*, Vienna 1910

FUMAGALLI 1960
G. Fumagalli, 'Gli "omini salvatichi" di Leonardo', *Raccolta Vinciana*, XVIII, 1960, pp. 129–57

GALLUZZI 1988
P. Galluzzi, *Leonardo e i proporzionanti* (XXVIII Lettura Vinciana), Florence 1988

GOLDSCHEIDER 1959
L. Goldscheider, *Leonardo da Vinci*, London 1959

GOMBRICH 1954
E. Gombrich, 'Leonardo's Grotesque Heads', in *Leonardo. Saggi e Ricerche*, ed. A. Marazza, Rome 1954, pp. 199–219, (reprinted in *The Heritage of Apelles*, London 1976, pp. 57–75)

GOMBRICH 1986
E. Gombrich, 'Ideal and Type in Italian Renaissance Painting', *New Light on Old Masters*, Oxford 1986, pp. 89–124

GOMBRICH AND KRIS 1952
E. Gombrich and E. Kris, 'The principles of caricature', in E. Kris, *Psychoanalytical Explorations in Art*, New York 1952, pp. 189–203

GOULD 1975
C. Gould, *Leonardo. The Artist and the Non-Artist*, London 1975

GREENBLATT 1980
S. Greenblatt, *Renaissance Self-fashioning*, Chicago 1980

GREGORI 1961
M. Gregori, 'Nuovi accertimenti in Toscana sulla pittura caricata e giocosa', *Arte Antica e Moderna*, XIII–XVI, 1961, pp. 400–416

HEMSOLL 1998
D. Hemsoll, 'Beauty as an aesthetic and artistic ideal in late fifteenth-century Florence', in *Concepts of Beauty in Renaissance Art*, ed. F. Ames-Lewis and M. Rogers, Aldershot 1998, pp. 66–79

HESS 1996
D. Hess, *Das Gothaer Liebespaar. Ein ungleiches Paar im Gewand höfischer Minne*, Frankfurt am Main 1996

HIND 1948
A.M. Hind, *Early Italian Engraving*,
7 vols, London 1948

JAFFÉ 1966
M. Jaffé, 'Rubens as a Collector of
Drawings, Part Three', *Master Drawings*,
IV, 1966, pp. 127–48

JAFFÉ 1994
M. Jaffé, *The Devonshire Collection of
Italian Drawings. Venetian and North
Italian Schools*, London 1994

KEELE AND PEDRETTI 1979
K. Keele and C. Pedretti, *Leonardo da
Vinci. Corpus of the Anatomical Studies in
the Collection of Her Majesty The Queen at
Windsor Castle*, 3 vols, London and New
York 1979

KELSO 1978
R. Kelso, *Doctrine for the Lady of the
Renaissance*, Urbana IL 1978

KEMP 1971
M. Kemp, '"Il concetto dell'anima" in
Leonardo's early skull studies', *Journal
of the Warburg and Courtauld Institutes*,
XXXIV, 1971, pp. 115–34

KEMP 1976
M. Kemp, 'Ogni dipintore dipinge sé:
A neoplatonic echo in Leonardo's art
theory?', in *Cultural Aspects of the Italian
Renaissance. Essays in Honour of Paul Oskar
Kristeller*, ed. C.H. Clough, Manchester
and New York 1976, pp. 311–23

KEMP 1981
M. Kemp, *Leonardo da Vinci. The
Marvellous Works of Nature and Man*,
London 1981

KEMP 1984–5
M. Kemp, 'Leonardo da Vinci: Science
and the Poetic Impulse', *Journal of the
Royal Society of Arts*, CXXXIII, 1984–5,
pp. 196–213

KEMP 1991
M. Kemp, 'Christo fanciullo', *Achademia
Leonardi Vinci*, IV, 1991, pp. 171–6

KEMP AND WALKER 1989
M. Kemp and M. Walker, *Leonardo on
Painting*, New Haven and London 1989

KNOX 2000
D. Knox, 'Civility, courtesy and women
in the Italian Renaissance', in *Women in
Italian Renaissance Culture and Society*, ed.
L. Panizza, Oxford 2000, pp. 2–17

KWAKKELSTEIN 1991
M. Kwakkelstein, 'Leonardo da Vinci's
grotesque heads and the breaking of
the physiognomic mould', *Journal of
the Warburg and Courtauld Institutes*, LIV,
1991, pp. 127–36

KWAKKELSTEIN 1993a
M. Kwakkelstein, 'Teste di vecchi in buon
numero', *Raccolta Vinciana*, XXV, 1993,
pp. 39–62

KWAKKELSTEIN 1993b
M. Kwakkelstein, 'The Lost Book on
"moti mentali"', *Achademia Leonardi
Vinci*, VI, 1993, pp. 56–66

KWAKKELSTEIN 1994
M. Kwakkelstein, *Leonardo da Vinci as
a Physiognomist. Theory and Drawing
Practice*, Leiden 1994

KWAKKELSTEIN 1998
M. Kwakkelstein, 'Botticelli, Leonardo,
and a Morris Dance', *Print Quarterly*, XV,
1998, pp. 4–14

LAURENZA 1996
D. Laurenza, 'La *fisionomia naturale* di
Leonardo: una traccia giovanile e alcuni
sviluppi', *Achademia Leonardi Vinci*, IX,
1996, pp. 14–19

LAURENZA 1997
D. Laurenza, '*Corpus mobile*. Tracce di
patognomica in Leonardo', *Raccolta
Vinciana*, XXVII, 1997, pp. 237–98

LEVI D'ANCONA 1977
M. Levi d'Ancona, *The Garden of the
Renaissance. Botanical Symbolism in Italian
Painting*, Florence 1977

LIMANTANI VIRDIS 1974
C. Limantani Virdis, 'Moralismo e
satira nella tarda produzione di Quinten
Metsys', *Storia dell'arte*, XX, 1974, pp. 25–35

LOMAZZO 1584
G.P. Lomazzo, *Trattato dell'arte della
pittura, scoltura, et architettura*, Milan 1584

LONDON 2000
*Sandro Botticelli. The Drawings to the
Divine Comedy*, exh. cat. by H.-Th.
Schulze Altcappenberg, London, Royal
Academy, 2000

LUGANO 1998
*Rabisch. Il grottesco nell'arte del
Cinquecento*, exh. cat., Lugano, Museo
Cantonale d'Arte, 1998

MCCONICA 1971
J. McConica, 'The Riddle of Terminus',
Erasmus in English, II, 1971, pp. 2–7

MCMAHON 1956
A.P. McMahon, *Treatise on Painting by
Leonardo da Vinci*, 2 vols, Princeton NJ
1956

MAGLI 1995
P. Magli, *Il volto e l'anima. Fisiognomica e
passioni*, Milan 1995

MANTUA 1994
Leon Battista Alberti, exh. cat., ed.
J. Rykwert and A. Engel, Mantua,
Palazzo Te, 1994

MANZONI 1881
G. Manzoni, *Studi di bibliografica
analitica. Studio primo*, Bologna 1881

MARANI 1986
P. Marani, *Disegni lombardi del Cinque
e Seicento della Pinacoteca di Brera e
dell'Arcivescovado di Milano*, Florence 1986

MARANI 1987
P. Marani, *Leonardo e i leonardeschi a
Brera*, Florence 1987

MARANI 1998
P. Marani, 'Ritratto di corte', in *Ambrogio
da Fossano detto il Bergognone*, ed. G.C.
Sciolla, Milan 1998, pp. 269–73

MARANI 2000
P. Marani, *Leonardo da Vinci. The Complete
Paintings*, New York 2000

MARINELLI 1981
S. Marinelli, 'The author of the Codex
Huygens', *Journal of the Warburg and
Courtauld Institutes*, XLIV, 1981, pp. 214–20

MARINONI 1989
A. Marinoni, 'Le proporzioni secondo
Leonardo', *Raccolta Vinciana*, XXIII, 1989,
pp. 259–73

MARINONI 1992
A. Marinoni, 'Figura donde diriva la
lussuria', *Raccolta Vinciana*, XXIV, 1992,
pp. 181–8

MEIJER 1971
B. Meijer, 'Esempi del comico figurativo
nel rinascimento lombardo', *Arte
Lombarda*, XVI, 1971, pp. 259–66

MEIJER 1998
B. Meijer, '"L'arte non deve schernire":
sul comico e sul grottesco al Nord', in
Lugano 1998, pp. 68–76

MELLER 1955
P. Meller, 'Leonardo da Vinci's Drawings
to the Divine Comedy', *Acta Historiae
Artium Academiae Scientiarum Hungaricae*,
II, 1955, pp. 135–66

MELLER 1963
P. Meller, 'Physiognomical theory in
Renaissance Heroic Portraits', in
*Studies in Western Art. Acts of the 20th
International Congress of the History of
Art*, Princeton NJ 1963, II, pp. 53–69

MELLER 1983
P. Meller, 'Quello che Leonardo non ha
scritto sulla figura umana: dall'Uomo di
Vitruvio alla Leda', *Arte Lombarda*, LXVII,
1983, pp. 117–33

MELLINKOFF 1993
R. Mellinkoff, *Outcasts. Signs of Otherness
in Northern European Art of the Late
Middle Ages*, Berkeley and Los Angeles
1993

MIEDEMA 1977
H. Miedema, 'Realism and comic mode:
the peasant', *Simiolus*, IX, 1977, pp. 205–19

MIGLIACCIO 1995
L. Migliaccio, 'Leonardo "auctor" del genere comico', *Achademia Leonardi Vinci*, VIII, 1995, pp. 158–61

MILAN 1982a
Leonardo all'Ambrosiana, exh. cat., ed. A. Marinoni and L. Cogliati Arano, Milan, Biblioteca Ambrosiana, 1982

MILAN 1982b
Zenale e Leonardo, exh. cat., Milan, Museo Poldi Pezzoli, 1982

MILAN 1984
Leonardo e l'incisione, exh. cat., ed. C. Alberici, Milan, Castello Sforzesco, 1984

MILAN 1987–8
Disegni e dipinti leonardeschi dalle collezioni milanesi, exh. cat., Milan, Palazzo Reale, 1987–8

MILAN 1998–9a
L'anima e il volto. Ritratto e fisiognomica da Leonardo a Bacon, exh. cat., ed. F. Caroli, Milan, Palazzo Reale, 1998–9

MILAN 1998–9b
L'Ambrosiana e Leonardo, exh. cat., Milan, Biblioteca-Pinacoteca Ambrosiana, 1998–9

MILAN 2001
Il Genio e le Passioni, exh. cat., ed. P. Marani, Milan, Palazzo Reale, 2001

MOCZULSKA 1995
K. Moczulska, 'The most graceful Gallerani and the most exquisite γαλεη in the portrait of Leonardo da Vinci', *Folia Historiae Artium*, I, 1995, pp. 77–86

MOFFITT 1994
J.F. Moffitt, '*Puer et Senex* in Didactic Contrapositum: Two Rhetorical Contexts for Leonardo's Grotesque Heads', *Achademia Leonardi Vinci*, VII, 1994, pp. 124–8

MONTAGU 1994
J. Montagu, *The Expression of the Passions. The Origin and Influence of Charles Le Brun's Conférence sur l'expression générale et particulière*, New Haven and London 1994

MOREL 1997
P. Morel, *Les Grotesques. Les figures de l'imaginaire dans la peinture italienne de la fin de la Renaissance*, Paris 1997

MUSACCHIO 2001
J.M. Musacchio, 'Weasels and pregnancy in Renaissance Italy', *Renaissance Studies*, XV, 2001, pp. 172–87

MUYLLE 1994
J. Muylle, 'Groteske koppen van Quinten Metsijs, Hieronymus Cock en Hans Liefrinck naar Leonardo da Vinci', *De zeventiende eeuw*, X, 1994, pp. 252–65

MUYLLE 2001
J. Muylle, 'Tronies toegeschreven aan Pieter Bruegel', *De zeventiende eeuw*, XVII, 2001, pp. 174–204

NEW YORK 1998–9
Heroic Armor of the Italian Renaissance. Filippo Negroli and his Contemporaries, exh. cat. by S. Pyhrr and J.-A. Godoy, New York, Metropolitan Museum of Art, 1998–9

ONIANS 1998
J. Onians, 'The biological basis of Renaissance aesthetics', in *Concepts of Beauty in Renaissance Art*, ed. F. Ames-Lewis and M. Rogers, Aldershot 1998, pp. 12–27

OST 1975
H. Ost, 'Leonardo als Steinschneider', *Leonardo-Studien*, Berlin and New York 1975, pp. 101–37

OST 1980
H. Ost, *Das Leonardo-Porträt in der Kgl Bibliothek Turin und andere Falschungen des Giuseppe Bossi*, Berlin 1980

PALIAGA 1995a
F. Paliaga, 'Giovanni Ambrogio Brambilla, "le teste di carattere" di Leonardo e la Commedia dell'Arte', *Raccolta Vinciana*, XXVI, 1995, pp. 219–54

PALIAGA 1995b
F. Paliaga, 'Quattro persone che ridono con un gatto', *Achademia Leonardi Vinci*, VII, 1995, pp. 143–57

PANOFSKY 1940
E. Panofsky, *The Codex Huygens and Leonardo da Vinci's Art Theory*, London 1940

PANOFSKY 1953
E. Panofsky, *Early Netherlandish Painting*, 2 vols, Cambridge MA 1953

PANOFSKY 1955
E. Panofsky, 'The History of the Theory of Human Proportion as a Reflection of the History of Styles', in *Meaning in the Visual Arts*, Garden City NY 1955, pp. 55–107

PANOFSKY 1969
E. Panofsky, 'Erasmus and the visual Arts', *Journal of the Warburg and Courtauld Institutes*, XXXII, 1969, pp. 200–27

PARRONCHI 1989
A. Parronchi, 'Nuove proposte per Leonardo scultore', *Achademia Leonardi Vinci*, II, 1989, pp. 40–67

PEDRETTI 1953
C. Pedretti, *Documenti e memorie riguardanti Leonardo da Vinci a Bologna e in Emilia*, Bologna 1953

PEDRETTI 1964
C. Pedretti, 'Dessins d'une scène, exécutés par Léonard de Vinci par Charles d'Amboise (1506–7)', in *Le Lieu Théâtral à la Renaissance*, ed. J. Jacquot, Paris 1964, pp. 27–34

PEDRETTI 1973
C. Pedretti, *Leonardo. A Study in chronology and style*, London 1973

PEDRETTI 1977
C. Pedretti, *The Literary Works of Leonardo da Vinci. A Commentary to Jean Paul Richter's Edition*, 2 vols, Oxford 1977

PEDRETTI 1983–6
C. Pedretti, *Studies for the Last Supper from the Royal Library at Windsor Castle*, exh. cat., Milan, Santa Maria delle Grazie and elsewhere, 1983–6

PEDRETTI 1984
C. Pedretti, 'L'altro Leonardo', in *Fra rinascimento, manierismo e realtà. Scritti di storia dell'arte in onore di Anna Maria Brizio*, ed. P. Marani, Florence 1984, pp. 17–30

PEDRETTI 1986
C. Pedretti, *Leonardo Architect*, London 1986

PEDRETTI 1987
C. Pedretti, *The Drawings and Miscellaneous Papers of Leonardo da Vinci in the Collection of Her Majesty The Queen at Windsor Castle. II: Horses and Other Animals*, London and New York 1987

PEDRETTI 1988a
C. Pedretti, 'Quae sunt Caesaris …', *Achademia Leonardi Vinci*, I, 1988, p. 121

PEDRETTI 1988b
C. Pedretti, 'Leonardo at the Morgan Library', *Achademia Leonardi Vinci*, I, 1988, pp. 142–4

PEDRETTI 1989
C. Pedretti, 'A Proem to Sculpture', *Achademia Leonardi Vinci*, II, 1989, pp. 11–39

PEDRETTI 1990a
C. Pedretti, 'The Spencer Grotesques', *Achademia Leonardi Vinci*, III, 1990, pp. 145–6

PEDRETTI 1990b
C. Pedretti, 'La Dama con l'ermellino come allegoria politica', *Studi politici in onore di Luigi Firpo*, eds. S. Rota Ghislandi and F. Barcia, Milan 1990, I, pp. 161–81

PEDRETTI 1991a
C. Pedretti, 'The Angel in the Flesh', *Achademia Leonardi Vinci*, IV, 1991, pp. 34–48

PEDRETTI 1991b
C. Pedretti, 'Il tema del profilo, o quasi', in *I leonardeschi a Milano*, ed. M.T. Fiorio and P. Marani, Milan 1991, pp. 14–23

PEDRETTI 1993
C. Pedretti, 'Daniello Bartoli e le
ricerche fisiognomiche di Leonardo',
Achademia Leonardi Vinci, VI, 1993,
pp. 145–53

PEDRETTI 1997
C. Pedretti, note in *Achademia Leonardi
Vinci*, X, 1997, p. 196

PENNINGTON 1982
R. Pennington, *A Descriptive Catalogue
of the Etched Work of Wenceslaus Hollar*,
Cambridge 1982

PLANISCIG 1927
L. Planiscig, 'Leonardos Porträte und
Aristoteles', in *Festschrift für Julius
Schlosser*, Vienna 1927, pp. 137–44

POPE-HENNESSY 1966
J. Pope-Hennessy, *The Portrait in the
Renaissance*, Princeton 1966

POPHAM 1946
A.E. Popham, *The Drawings of Leonardo
da Vinci*, London 1946

POPHAM 1954
A.E. Popham, 'The Dragon-Fight', in
Leonardo. Saggi e Ricerche, ed. A. Marazza,
Rome 1954, pp. 223–7

POUNCEY AND GERE 1962
P. Pouncey and J. Gere, *Italian Drawings
in the Department of Prints and Drawings
at the British Museum. Raphael and his
Circle*, 2 vols, London 1962

PUPPI 1993
L. Puppi, '*Leonardo & Venezia*: un
"pasticciaccio brutto" a Palazzo Grassi',
Venezia arti, VII, 1993, pp. 124–8

REBHORN 1978
W. Rebhorn, *Courtly Performances.
Masking and Festivity in Castiglione's Book
of the Courtier*, Detroit 1978

RETI 1968
L. Reti, 'The Two Unpublished
Manuscripts of Leonardo da Vinci in the
Biblioteca Nacional of Madrid – II',
Burlington Magazine, CX, 1968, pp. 81–9

RICHTER 1939
J.P. Richter, *The Literary Works of
Leonardo da Vinci*, 2nd edn, 2 vols,
Oxford 1939

ROBERTS (FORTHCOMING)
J. Roberts, 'Thomas Howard, the
collector Earl of Arundel, and
Leonardo's drawings', in *The Evolution of
English Collecting*, New Haven and
London

ROGERS 1988
M. Rogers, 'The decorum of women's
beauty', *Renaissance Studies*, II (1), 1988,
pp. 47–89

ROGERS 1998
M. Rogers, 'The artist as beauty', in
Concepts of Beauty in Renaissance Art, eds
F. Ames-Lewis and M. Rogers, Aldershot
1998, pp. 93–106

ROME 1998–9
Leonardo. La dama con l'ermellino, exh.
cat., eds B. Fabjan and P. Marani, Rome,
Palazzo del Quirinale, 1998–9

ROTTERDAM 1969
Erasmus en zijn tijd, exh. cat., Rotterdam,
Museum Boymans-van Beuningen, 1969

ROWLANDS 1980
J. Rowlands, 'Terminus, the Device of
Erasmus of Rotterdam: A Painting by
Holbein', *Bulletin of the Cleveland Museum
of Art*, LXVII, 1980, pp. 50–54

RUBIN 1990
P. Rubin, 'What men saw. Vasari's life of
Leonardo da Vinci and the image of the
Renaissance artist', *Art History*, XIII, 1990,
pp. 34–46

SASLOW 1986
J.M. Saslow, *Ganymede in the Renaissance.
Homosexuality in Art and Society*, New
Haven and London 1986

SCAGLIA 1982
G. Scaglia, 'Leonardo's non-inverted
writing and Verrocchio's measured
drawing of a horse', *Art Bulletin*, XLIV,
1982, pp. 31–44

SCHOFIELD 1992
R. Schofield, 'Avoiding Rome: An
introduction to Lombard sculptors and
the antique', *Arte Lombarda*, C, 1992,
pp. 29–44

SCHOFIELD 1997
R. Schofield, 'The Medallions of the
Basamento of the Certosa di Pavia:
Sources and Influences', *Arte Lombarda*,
CXX, 1997, pp. 5–27

SCOTT-ELLIOT 1958
A. Scott-Elliot, 'Caricature heads after
Leonardo da Vinci in the Spencer
Collection', *Bulletin of the New York Public
Library*, LXII, 1958, pp. 277–99

SHEARMAN 1978
J. Shearman, 'The Galerie François
Premier: A Case in Point', *Miscellanea
Musicologica (Adelaide Studies in
Musicology)*, II, 1978, pp. 1–16

SHELL AND SIRONI 1991
J. Shell and G. Sironi, 'Salaì and
Leonardo's legacy', *Burlington Magazine*,
CXXXIII, 1991, pp. 95–108

SHELL AND SIRONI 1992
J. Shell and G. Sironi, 'Salaì and the
inventory of his estate', *Raccolta
Vinciana*, XXIV, 1992, pp. 109–53

SHIRLEY 1968
J. Shirley, ed. and trans., *A Parisian
Journal, 1405–1449*, Oxford 1968

SILVER 1974
L. Silver, 'The Ill-Matched Pair by
Quinten Massys', *Studies in the History
of Art*, VI, 1974, pp. 104–23

SILVER 1977
L. Silver, 'Power and pelf: A new-found
Old man by Massys', *Simiolus*, IX, 1977,
pp. 63–92

SILVER 1978
L. Silver, 'Prayer and Laughter:
Erasmian Elements in two late Massys
panels', *Erasmus in English*, IX, 1978,
pp. 17–21

SILVER 1984
L. Silver, *The Paintings of Quinten Massys
with a Catalogue Raisonné*, Oxford 1984

SIMONS 1988
P. Simons, 'Women in Frames: The
Gaze, the Eye, the Profile in Renaissance
Portraiture', *History Workshop Journal*,
XXV, 1988, pp. 4–30

SINGLETON 1936
C. Singleton, ed., *Canti carnascialeschi
del Rinascimento*, Bari 1936

SOLMI 1924
E. Solmi, *Scritti vinciani*, Florence 1924

STEINBERG 1973
L. Steinberg, 'Leonardo's Last Supper',
Art Quarterly, XXXVI, 1973, pp. 297–410

STEINITZ 1949
K. Steinitz, 'A reconstruction of
Leonardo da Vinci's revolving stage',
Art Quarterly, XII, 1949, pp. 325–38

STEINITZ 1958
K. Steinitz, 'Les décors de théâtre de
Léonard de Vinci: Paradis et Enfer',
Bibliothèque d'Humanisme et Renaissance,
XX, 1958, pp. 257–65

STEINITZ 1964
K. Steinitz, 'Le dessin de Léonard de
Vinci pour la représentation de la Danaë
de Baldassare Taccone', in *Le Lieu
Théâtral à la Renaissance*, ed. J. Jacquot,
Paris 1964, pp. 35–40

STEINITZ 1970
K. Steinitz, *Leonardo architetto teatrale
e organizzatore di feste* (IX Lettura
Vinciana), Florence 1970

STEINITZ 1974
K. Steinitz, *Pierre Jean Mariette, le Comte
de Caylus and their Concept of Leonardo
da Vinci in the Eighteenth Century*,
Los Angeles 1974

STEWART 1977
A. Stewart, *Unequal Lovers. A Study
of Unequal Couples in Northern Art*,
New York 1977

SUIDA 1929
W. Suida, *Leonardo und sein Kreis*,
Munich 1929

SUIDA 1941
W. Suida, 'A Leonardo Profile and Dynamism in Portraiture', *Art in America*, XXIX, 1941, pp. 62–72

SUIDA 1949
W. Suida, 'Again the Simonetta Bust', *Art Quarterly*, XII, 1949, pp. 176–8

SUMMERS 1981
D. Summers, *Michelangelo and the Language of Art*, Princeton 1981

TIETZE-CONRAT 1957
E. Tietze-Conrat, *Dwarfs and Jesters in Art*, London 1957

TINAGLI 1997
P. Tinagli, *Women in Italian Renaissance Art. Gender, Representation, Identity*, Manchester and New York 1997

TRAVERSI 1997
L. Traversi, 'Il tema dei "Due fanciulli che si baciano e abbracciano" tra "Leonardismo italiano" e "Leonardismo fiammingo"', *Raccolta Vinciana*, XXVII, 1997, pp. 373–437

TRUTTY-COOHILL 1993a
P. Trutty-Coohill, *The Drawings of Leonardo da Vinci and his Circle in America*, Florence 1993

TRUTTY-COOHILL 1993b
P. Trutty-Coohill, 'The Spencer Collection of Grotesques and Caricatures after Leonardo', *Arte Lombarda*, CV–CVII, 1993, pp. 48–54

TRUTTY-COOHILL 1997
P. Trutty-Coohill, 'Making the Dead Laugh', *Achademia Leonardi Vinci*, X, 1997, pp. 190–96

TURNER 1993
A.R. Turner, *Inventing Leonardo*, New York 1993

VALENTINER 1937
W.R. Valentiner, 'Leonardo's portrait of Beatrice d'Este', *Art in America and Elsewhere*, XXV, 1937, pp. 3–23

VALLESE 1992
G. Vallese, 'Leonardo's *Malinchonia*', *Achademia Leonardi Vinci*, X, 1992, pp. 43–51

VANDENBROECK 1987
P. Vandenbroeck, *Beeld van de andere, vertoog over het zelf: over wilden en narren, boeren en bedelaars*, Antwerp 1987

VASARI 1965
G. Vasari, *Lives of the Artists*, ed. and trans. G. Bull, London 1965

VENICE 1992
Leonardo and Venice, exh. cat., ed. P. Marani, Venice, Palazzo Grassi, 1992

VERTOVA 1992
L. Vertova, 'La barba di Leonardo', in *Nuove ricerche in margine alla mostra: Da Leonardo a Rembrandt. Atti del Convegno Internazionale di Studi*, Turin 1992, pp. 15–23

VIATTE 1994
F. Viatte, 'Verrocchio et Leonardo da Vinci: à propos des têtes idéales', in *Florentine Drawing at the Time of Lorenzo the Magnificent*, ed. E. Cropper, Bologna 1994, pp. 45–53

VINCI 1997
L'immagine di Leonardo, exh cat., ed. R.P. Ciardi and C. Sisi, Vinci, Palazzina Uzielli, 1997

VINCI 2001
Leonardo e il mito di Leda, exh. cat., ed. D. Dalli Regoli *et al.*, Vinci, Palazzina Uzielli, 2001

VISCONTI 1979
G. Visconti, *I canzonieri per Beatrice d'Este e per Bianca Maria Sforza*, ed. P. Bongrani, Milan 1979

WASHINGTON 2001–2
Virtue and Beauty. Leonardo's Ginevra de' Benci and Renaissance Portraits of Women, exh. cat., ed. D.A. Brown, Washington, National Gallery of Art, 2001–2

WASSERMAN 1974
J. Wasserman, review of Clark and Pedretti 1968–9, *Burlington Magazine*, CXVI, 1974, pp. 111–13

WASSERMAN 1975
J. Wasserman, 'The Monster Leonardo Painted for his Father', in *Art Studies for an Editor. 25 Essays in Memory of Milton S. Fox*, New York 1975, pp. 261–7

WEISS 1968
R. Weiss, 'The Study of Ancient Numismatics during the Renaissance (1313–1517)', *Numismatic Chronicle*, VIII, 1968, pp. 177–87

WIND 1937–8
E. Wind, 'Aenigma Termini', *Journal of the Warburg Institute*, I, 1937–8, pp. 66–9

WIND 1998
B. Wind, *A Foul and Pestilential Congregation. Images of 'Freaks' in Baroque Art*, Aldershot and Brookfield VT 1998

WINTERNITZ 1974
E. Winternitz, 'Leonardo and Music', in *The Unknown Leonardo*, ed. L. Reti, Maidenhead 1974, pp. 110–34

WOODS-MARSDEN 1998
J. Woods-Marsden, *Renaissance Self-Portraiture*, New Haven and London 1998

WOODS-MARSDEN 2001–2
J. Woods-Marsden, 'Portrait of the Lady, 1430–1520', in Washington 2001–2, pp. 63–87

ZÖLLNER 1985
F. Zöllner, 'Agrippa, Leonardo and the Codex Huygens', *Journal of the Warburg and Courtauld Institutes*, XLVIII, 1985, pp. 229–34

ZÖLLNER 1987
F. Zöllner, *Vitruvs Proportionsfigur. Quellenkritische Studien zur Kunstliteratur im 15. und 16. Jahrhundert*, Worms 1987

ZÖLLNER 1989
F. Zöllner, 'Die Bedeutung von Codex Huygens und Codex Urbinas für die Proportions- und Bewegungsstudien Leonardos da Vinci', *Zeitschrift für Kunstgeschichte*, LII, 1989, pp. 334–52

ZÖLLNER 1992
F. Zöllner, 'Ogni Pittore Dipinge Sè: Leonardo da Vinci and Automimesis', in *Der Künstler über sich in seinem Werk*, ed. M. Winner, Weinheim 1992, pp. 137–60

ZÖLLNER 1993
F. Zöllner, 'Leonardo's Portrait of Mona Lisa del Giocondo', *Gazette des Beaux-Arts*, CXXI, 1993, pp. 115–38

ZÖLLNER 1995
F. Zöllner, 'L'uomo vitruviano di Leonardo da Vinci, Rudolf Wittkower e l'*Angelus Novus* di Walter Benjamin', *Raccolta Vinciana*, XXVI, 1995, pp. 329–58

ZOUBOV 1960
V.P. Zoubov, 'Léon-Battista Alberti et Léonard de Vinci', *Raccolta Vinciana*, XVIII, 1960, pp. 1–14

CONCORDANCE

WITH ROYAL LIBRARY INVENTORY NUMBERS

RL 12276	CAT. 1	RL 12492	CAT. 39	RL 12553	CAT. 19
RL 12294	CAT. 8	RL 12493	CAT. 38	RL 12554	CAT. 17
RL 12318	CAT. 6	RL 12494	CAT. 21	RL 12555V	CAT. 26
RL 12319	CAT. 7	RL 12495	CAT. 41	RL 12556	CAT. 20
RL 12326	CAT. 47	RL 12498	CAT. 42	RL 12557	CAT. 18
RL 12327	CAT. 48	RL 12499	CAT. 24	RL 12567	CAT. 9
RL 12329	CAT. 71	RL 12500	CAT. 25	RL 12574	CAT. 73
RL 12367	CAT. 64	RL 12502	CAT. 22	RL 12575	CAT. 72
RL 12369	CAT. 65	RL 12503	CAT. 23	RL 12577	CAT. 74
RL 12370	CAT. 62	RL 12505	CAT. 43	RL 12585	CAT. 70
RL 12371	CAT. 63	RL 12508	CAT. 75	RL 12587	CAT. 49
RL 12432	CAT. 16	RL 12512	CAT. 45	RL 12588	CAT. 68
RL 12448	CAT. 29	RL 12513	CAT. 44	RL 12589	CAT. 66
RL 12449	CAT. 40	RL 12515	CAT. 60	RL 12590	CAT. 69
RL 12453	CAT. 36	RL 12516	CAT. 58	RL 12593	CAT. 10
RL 12457	CAT. 33	RL 12517	CAT. 61	RL 12594	CAT. 11
RL 12459	CAT. 32	RL 12518	CAT. 59	RL 12596	CAT. 12
RL 12461	CAT. 67	RL 12519	CAT. 15	RL 12601	CAT. 4
RL 12462	CAT. 34	RL 12533	CAT. 56	RL 12726	CAT. 46
RL 12463	CAT. 35	RL 12534	CAT. 57	RL 19000V	CAT. 13
RL 12474	CAT. 31	RL 12547	CAT. 54	RL 19012	CAT. 14
RL 12488	CAT. 30	RL 12548	CAT. 53	RL 19055V	CAT. 50
RL 12489	CAT. 28	RL 12550	CAT. 55	RL 19057	CAT. 5
RL 12490	CAT. 27	RL 12551	CAT. 52	RL 19132	CAT. 2
RL 12491	CAT. 37	RL 12552	CAT. 51	RL 19136–9V	CAT. 3

INDEX